(THAT SUBTILE WREATH)

LECTURES PRESENTED AT THE QUATERCENTENARY CELEBRATION OF THE BIRTH OF JOHN DONNE

Edited by Margaret W. Pepperdene

Inaugurating the James Ross McCain Lecture Series

Agnes Scott College

1972

Illustration of Donne by Erin Sherman, Class of 1973,
Agnes Scott College

FOREWORD

On February 24-25, 1972, the Quatercentenary Celebration of the birth of John Donne was held at Agnes Scott College. For the occasion, we were delighted to have on our campus colleagues and students from colleges and universities in the Atlanta area and seventeenth century scholars from all over the country. From the time that we on the English faculty of the College began to plan this Celebration, the most enthusiastic participant in the undertaking was President Wallace M. Alston, who has been responsible during his tenure of office for bringing to this campus many poets, novelists, and literary scholars of the highest merit. It was he who suggested that the lectures to be presented at the Quatercentenary Celebration inaugurate the James Ross McCain Lecture Series, established in honor of the distinguished former president of the College. As a result, the Celebration took on an additional dimension of importance to the College.

The Celebration was a memorable twenty-four hours for all of us who shared it. The scholarly significance of the lectures presented, the beauty of the musical program, and the festive spirit engendered by the occasion created a joyous "anniversarie." The focus of the Celebration was the three lectures presented by Professor Frank Manley of Emory University, who is the editor of Donne's *Anniversaries*, Professor Louis L. Martz of Yale University, who has done some of the most significant recent scholarship on Donne and whose book, *The Poetry of Meditation*, is a seminal study, and Professor Patricia G. Pinka, a promising

i

young Donne scholar on our own faculty. As President Alston said in his welcoming address to the participants and guests, these lectures are "worthy to be preserved and shared." We are pleased to present them in this volume.

In the first lecture, "Formal Wit in the *Songs and Sonnets*," Professor Manley, in a sensitive and penetrating analysis of "The Sunne Rising" and "The Anniversarie," shows how Donne by the use of formal wit, that is, wit within the form of the poem itself, sets the stereotyped subject matter of the traditional genre on its head and in so doing reverses the original purpose of the genre. Using the traditional subject matter of the *alba* in "The Sunne Rising," Donne turns the poem from the usual lament for the loss of a night of love to a celebration of love as the only reality of life. Manley also suggests that Donne uses wit in the same way in "The Anniversarie," turning the *epitaphia anniversarium*, an annual poem honoring the dead, into a poem celebrating life.

Professor Martz's scholarly career is intimately connected with Donne's *Anniversaries*. It began with an essay on the poems which later developed into his most influential book, *The Poetry of Meditation*. In the present lecture, "Donne's *Anniversaries* Revisited," Professor Martz returns to the *Anniversaries* and offers a reading of the poems which incorporates the major findings of recent criticism as well as his own reflections on the poems since he first called attention to them twenty-five years ago. As Frank Manley has said, "It is rare for one man to have the good fortune to call the attention of the world to a neglected masterpiece. It is even rarer to have the further good fortune to be able to reassess that discovery in the light of later knowledge and strike out new directions for the future."

For inclusion in this volume and as a complement to his lecture Professor Martz has prepared "A Selected Bibliography of Writings on Donne's *Anniversaries*," which is of inestimable value to students of these poems.

In the third lecture, "The Autobiographical Narrator in the *Songs and Sonnets*," Professor Pinka in an analysis of "The Relique" and "Farewell to Love" shows how the involved narrator of these poems manipulates his fiction in order to influence the listener. She has taken the narrator's point of view, his relationship to his listener, his concern with the past and future, and his rejection of the present and demonstrated the way in which Donne has interwoven these to modify meaning and to develop levels of meaning within the poems.

We have included also in this volume the program of seventeenth century music set to Donne's lyrics which was presented at the Celebration. The illustration of the manuscript of Donne's "Goe and catch a fallinge star," (BM MS. Egerton 2013, f. 58ᵛ) opposite the program of music is published with the permission of the British Library Board.

Margaret W. Pepperdene
Department of English
Agnes Scott College

September, 1973

CONTENTS

WELCOMING ADDRESS

WALLACE M. ALSTON
President, Agnes Scott College

This is a very happy occasion for us at Agnes Scott College and one we have anticipated with excitement and pleasure. It is my special privilege to welcome to our campus our distinguished participants and the many guests who have joined us in this Quatercentenary Celebration of the birth of John Donne. The focus of this celebration is a series of lectures by Professor Louis L. Martz of Yale University, Professor Frank Manley of Emory University, and Professor Patricia G. Pinka of the English faculty of Agnes Scott College. There will also be a program of seventeenth century music set to Donne's lyrics and performed by Miss Sally Martin, a student at Agnes Scott, and Mr. Lou Aull, lutenist. I understand, also, that the students have planned a special birthday party at the reception this evening following Mr. Martz's lecture. We want this to be a festive and joyous occasion for all of you.

The lectures to be presented are particularly appropriate to initiate the lecture series at Agnes Scott honoring the former president of this College, Dr. James Ross McCain. The James Ross McCain Lecture Series was established as one means of keeping alive the memory and the influence of this unusual man. Those who were responsible for providing the funds and setting up the Lecture Series described their purpose in this statement:

. . . to provide a lecture or series of lectures on some aspect
of the liberal arts and sciences with reference to the religious
dimensions of human life.

This celebration of the life of John Donne, poet and divine, seems a most fitting way to fulfill the purpose of the James Ross McCain Lecture Series.

Dr. McCain's influence as an educator and as a Christian layman has been many-faceted and far-reaching. For fifty years he was an integral part of the life of Agnes Scott College. From 1915 to 1923 he served on the faculty of history and in various capacities in the administration. From 1923 until his retirement in 1951 at the age of seventy, he was President of the College; from 1951 until his death in 1965 he was chairman of the Executive Committee of the Board of Trustees of the College. As a leading Presbyterian layman he was active throughout his life in the service of his church, and in 1951 he was named Moderator of the Presbyterian Church in the United States.

His influence as an educator extended beyond this campus to both the region and the nation. He is generally recognized as one of the pioneers in setting academic standards in southern higher education. As a member of the Executive Committee of the Southern Association of Colleges and Schools he was instrumental in establishing standards for accreditation and in forming the Commission on Colleges to examine and accredit colleges and universities in the southern region. In 1935 he helped found the Southern University Conference to improve the quality of higher education. His leadership was a major factor in establishing the University Center in Georgia, which secured financial support from national foundations for faculty research. Older members of faculties in the colleges and universities of Georgia well remember that it was Dr. McCain who led the Southern Association in its fight for academic freedom in this state. National recognition as an educator came to Dr. McCain with his election as president of the Association of American Colleges and as a Senator of the United Chapters of Phi Beta Kappa. From 1940 to 1946 he was a Trustee of the General Education Board of the Rockefeller Foundation. His valuable services to higher education were recognized by honorary degrees granted to him by Emory University, University of Chattanooga, Davidson College, Erskine College, and Tulane University.

The James Ross McCain Lecture Series has been established at Agnes Scott to honor both the man and the academic excellence he believed in. This symposium honoring the 400th anniversary of the birth of John Donne and inaugurating the James Ross McCain Lectures celebrates a happy union from which will come lectures that are worthy of being preserved and shared.

February 24, 1972

Frank Manley

FORMAL WIT IN THE *SONGS AND SONNETS*

When I was an undergraduate at Emory and my wife was still a student at Agnes Scott, there was a professor here you may have heard your mothers or your aunts talk about. He was loved and admired by generations of students in the College for his kindliness and cantankerousness and the wisdom of his years.* One of the courses this professor taught was a course in Donne, and one of the things he did in this course to amuse himself and instruct the young ladies in his charge was to emphasize all the explicit, erotic passages in the love poems, analyzing them in great detail. After going through a good bit of Donne in this way, the students were asked to write a paper on "The Relique." The young ladies dutifully went through the poem in the accustomed fashion, explaining exactly what Donne meant by the little stay the lovers would make beside the grave at the last, busy day, when they got their bodies back again. They would linger over the very fine, erotic image of the bracelet of bright hair about the bone, talk about the link between woman-head and maidenhead, Mary Magdalene's previous occupation, and so on—the seals on the sex organs, the ironic miracle, and the man's over-all impatience with the woman. Then, after the papers had been handed in, the professor would explain that that is not what Donne meant at all. The miracle of their love, he would say, was Platonic. There was something supranatural about it, like the gleams of unearthly light Ficino says we sometimes perceive in the beauty of those we love. He would stress the sense of awe and wonder in the last stanza:

> First, we lov'd well and faithfully,
> Yet knew not what wee lov'd, nor why,
> Difference of sex no more wee knew,
> Then our Guardian Angells doe;
> > Comming and going, wee
> Perchance might kisse, but not between those meales;
> > Our hands ne'r toucht the seales,
> Which nature, injur'd by late law, sets free:
> These miracles wee did; but now alas,
> All measure, and all language, I should passe,
> Should I tell what a miracle shee was.[1]

And of course the professor was right. The exercise was a witty one that caught the students up short and hopefully taught them something about reading Donne. But I have always suspected that the ladies were also right, for the poem is in some sense a *carpe diem* poem. The *carpe diem* tradition is usually used in Western literature to convince a young woman that she should make use of her beauty and youth while she still has them, before they are destroyed by the inexorable passage of time. "Dum loquimur," Horace wrote, "fugerit invidia / Aetas: carpe diem, quam minimum credula postero."[2] (Even while we are talking, envious time is running: seize today—*carpe diem*—and trust nothing to tomorrow.) "For at my back," Marvell would add,

> I alwaies hear
> Times winged Charriot hurrying near:
> And yonder all before us lye
> Desarts of vast Eternity.[3]

In "The Relique" Donne holds the lady's head over the grave in the first stanza and asks her to look and tell him what she sees in store for them:

> When my grave is broke up againe
> Some second ghest to entertaine,
> (For graves have learn'd that woman-head
> To be to more then one a Bed)
> And he that digs it, spies
> A bracelet of bright haire about the bone,
> Will he not let'us alone,
> And thinke that there a loving couple lies,
> Who thought that this device might be some way
> To make their soules, at the last busie day,
> Meet at this grave, and make a little stay?
>
> (p. 89)

This vision of the grave dominates the rest of the poem; and if it is not intended to urge the lady to make use of her youth and beauty now while there is still time, it at least allows her sensual lover to express his own opinion of the affair. In the third stanza, however, the *carpe diem* motif is combined in a very strange way with what seems to be a celebration of Platonic love, and in the tension and ambiguity that results it is difficult to say whether the miracle in the last few lines is true or false, serious or ironic—whether, that is, the supranatural relationship of the lovers is a good or a good that carries with it something so abnormal and unnatural that the speaker regards it with a kind of ironic loathing mixed with the wonder and awe:

> These miracles wee did; but now alas,
> All measure, and all language, I should passe,
> Should I tell what a miracle shee was.
>
> (p. 90)

And that is what I want to talk about this afternoon—the way in which Donne took certain traditional lyric genres defined not by metrical form but content, and by a sudden flash of wit turned them upside-down so that while remaining recognizably themselves, they became the vehicles for an entirely new and original experience. In using these forms, Donne revivifies them, or at least the essential impulse that gave rise to them in the first place, but he also makes them over into something uniquely his own.

Donne's poem "The Baite," for example, is a pastoral invitation. In the invitation a shepherd usually asks a shepherdess to come with him and be his love, and he offers her various gifts to entice her. Marlowe's "Passionate Shepherd to his Love" is the best known example in English. It was answered by Raleigh in his palinode, "The Nymph's Reply," which cynically responds to the invitation line by line, bursting the pastoral illusion. Donne's poem begins with Marlowe's first line and is usually taken to be a parody like Raleigh's, but it is actually an invitation in its own right, only with a new twist. Donne offers the lady not the usual gifts, but a new experience. He offers to take her fishing and swimming, and the poem ends up not as an invitation, but as a definition of love in which the lady herself is the major metaphor:

Let coarse bold hands, from slimy nest
The bedded fish in banks out-wrest,
Or curious traitors, sleave-silke flies
Bewitch poore fishes wandring eyes.

For thee, thou needst no such deceit,
For thou thy selfe art thine owne bait,
That fish, that is not catch'd thereby,
Alas, is wiser farre then I.

(p. 33)

8

"Twicknam Garden" is a *reverdie* or song of the awakening of spring. "The Curse" is a variant of the classical *dirae*, and the "Song: 'Goe, and catche a falling starre,'" the *adunata* or catalogue of impossibilities, combined perhaps with the Provençal poem of obscure statement, the *devinalh*. "The Canonization" is a *tenso* or *débat d'amour* placed in a dramatic context. And so on. There are *carpe diem* poems, *albas* or *aubades, epitaphia recens, epitaphia anniversaria*, and the form most characteristic of Donne, the song of the parting of lovers, which he calls the *valediction*.

The only difficulty is that most of these lyric genres are now forgotten, and we are unable to enjoy therefore as fully as we should the brilliance and audacity with which Donne handles these stereotyped situations, ringing changes on them with what I have referred to in the title of this lecture as a formal wit—a wit, that is, located within the form of the poem itself. What I would like to do this afternoon is consider two of these forgotten lyric types and see what use Donne made of them.

The first is the *alba* or dawn song. The origins of the form are obscure. Intimations appear in classical lyrics, such as certain of Ovid's *Amores*,[4] but it is not until the celebrated bilingual *alba* of the tenth century[5] that we arrive at a formal literary type, which shortly thereafter became stereotyped in the poetry of Provençe. The situation is always the same. Two lovers have enjoyed a night of stolen pleasure together, but now the morning approaches. They hear the songs of birds or the *guetteur* in the tower of the castle, crying the watches of the night. The poem takes place at that moment, in the half-light of dawn, and it catches in its quality of bittersweet lament some imitation of that time of day. The enjoyment of the night is not yet fully over, but the coming of day has already touched the lovers with sorrow.

At its best the *alba* is not only a lament for the loss of a night of love. It is a lament for the passing of all the moments of heightened existence in our lives and the impermanence and imperfection of human happiness and contentment. For the demands of the world and our daytime existence are harsh. The lovers are grateful for what they have had, but they know that it cannot be prolonged. They accept their nature and the world they live in, the alternation of days and nights in their lives, because they realize that the night and the pleasure they found within it are like a dream. The duties and responsibilities of the day, however, and the routine of their ordinary lives are real. Much as they are saddened by this, they accept it unthinkingly, and as the poem ends, the night and the love it gave them are gone.

One of the difficulties in writing an *alba* is the need to vary the content slightly so as to make it new while still retaining the contours of the old. In *Romeo and Juliet*, for example, Shakespeare has the lovers spend the first night of their marriage together, and when they wake in the morning they argue whether the bird they hear singing is a lark, the sign of day, or the nightingale:

Juliet: Wilt thou be gone? It is not yet near day.
          It was the nightingale, and not the lark,
          That pierced the fearful hollow of thine ear.

               . . .

Romeo: It was the lark, the herald of the morn,
          No nightingale. Look, love, what envious streaks
          Do lace the severing clouds in yonder east.
          Night's candles are burnt out, and jocund day
          Stands tiptoe on the misty mountaintops.
          I must be gone and live, or stay and die.[6]

10

Shakespeare varied the form of the *alba* by having the lovers married but still unable to be together and by combining the form with the medieval *conflictus* or *débat*, in which two birds usually carry on a debate, with the poetry imitating the sound of their song. Modern variations are somewhat more extreme, as in W. D. Snodgrass' "Vampire's Aubade." The vampire speaks, echoing Suckling:

> Why so drawn, so worn,
> My dearest;
> Should this sun-drenched morn
> Find you so burned out and so pale?
> Until now I've had no fear lest
> *You'd* be quick to fail.[7]

William Empson also has an *alba*, in which the lovers are awakened by an earthquake:

> Hours before dawn we were woken by the quake.
> My house was on a cliff. The thing could take
> Bookloads of shelves, break bottles in a row.
> Then the long pause and then the bigger shake.
> It seemed the best thing to be up and go.[8]

Donne himself wrote three *albas*—"The Sunne Rising," "The Good-morrow," and the "Breake of Day"—and possibly one other that Miss Gardner places among the poems of doubtful attribution.

In "The Sunne Rising," a lover who has spent a night of pleasure in bed with his lady is awakened by the sun shining into the room, and the poem begins with a burst of anger:

11

> Busie old foole, unruly Sunne,
>   Why dost thou thus,
> Through windowes, and through curtaines call on us?
> Must to thy motions lovers seasons run?
>   (p. 72)

The first movement of the poem consists essentially of a contrast between the way the lover regards himself and the way he regards the rest of the world. Much of what goes on at the beginning is fully understandable only after we have participated in the poem long enough to understand the speaker's peculiar point of view. For the speaker himself is not yet fully aware of what he is saying except in an emotional, subliminal way, present in the metaphor he chooses to describe himself and the abstract boast he makes about love at the end of the stanza. In more than one sense the poem is an awakening, not only in bed after a night of love, but an awakening into full consciousness of what one truly is and what in love one truly possesses.

The metaphor the speaker chooses for himself is that of a king or great lord. The sun is an old fool, a bumbling servant kept around the house for old time's sake long after his useful years have passed. In waking his lord and lady this early, he has made a serious mistake, and the speaker addresses him in tones of aristocratic arrogance and chastisement. The operative word here is the word *unruly* in the first line. To apply it to the sun, the source of all our light and all our vitality, is considerably ironic, for the sun is the most "ruly" thing in our unruly lives. It rises and sets according to its own inexorable schedule, inflexible as fate. The speaker does not quite seem to have taken that into account as yet, except in terms of the metaphor itself.

After his initial outburst of anger, the speaker then explains to the sun precisely where his duties lie:

12

> Sawcy pedantique wretch, goe chide
> Late schoole boyes, and sowre prentices,
> Goe tell Court-huntsmen, that the King will ride,
> Call countrey ants to harvest offices.
>
> (p. 72)

Notice the categories chosen: all are ruled and obsessed by time—young children hurried along to school by their pedagogue, teenage apprentices sour with yesterday's sweat, courtiers seeking the favor of the king, who hunt when he hunts, a colony of ants instinctively rushing in all directions at once to lay up supplies before the winter sets in. All are hurried, all are late and anxious, totally dependent on the authority of someone or something outside themselves. The catalogue is also a microcosm of city and country (the urban scenes of schoolboys and apprentices as opposed to the rural scenes of hunting and harvest) as well as the various seasons of the year, from winter to autumn. The entire world, Donne suggests, is obsessed by time. Only the lovers in the still point of their bed are free, dependent on nothing outside their love. The sun, therefore, has no control over them:

> Love, all alike, no season knowes, nor clyme,
> Nor houres, dayes, months, which are the rags of time.
>
> (p. 72)

At this point in the poem this is a statement only. It has not yet been experienced or proved. It is not even fully articulate. The metaphor of the rags of time, for example, is almost completely submerged, as though the speaker were only half-conscious of what he is saying. But the implications are extremely important, for the metaphor seems to say that time is something other than its measurement: that we perceive only the accidents of time in

13

the vicissitudes of hours, days, months, whereas time itself in its essential nature is changeless, never varying, like a constant burning light. The speaker sees all this as through a glass darkly, not yet fully aware of what he is saying. He is conscious only of his own exasperation that the night of love is over and that the world and its responsibilities beckon.

The second stanza begins with an abrupt shift in attitude. The sunlight falling in the room is no longer regarded as saucy and unruly, but reverend and strong:

> Thy beames, so reverend, and strong
> Why shouldst thou thinke?
> I could eclipse and cloud them with a winke,
> But that I would not lose her sight so long.
> (p. 72)

I know you are there, he says to the sun. I know what I said about love being all alike and so on. We lovers think we are untouched by time, but all the while something is always standing beside the bed with a watch in its hand. We can close our eyes and ignore it, but it does not really change things. By this time all the strength and mastery of the speaker have drained from him, and we are left with the intellectual juggler, who does not really care what he says so long as it works. The argument is flashy; it sounds good; but it is not entirely convincing. And neither is the argument in the second turn of the stanza, which again produces the opposite effect from the one intended. Once again the speaker tacitly admits the power of the sun in the very act of denying it. Since you see what a treasure I have here in bed, he says to the sun, you had better go check and see if the East and West Indies, your treasuries of spices and gold, are still where you left them:

14

If her eyes have not blinded thine,
    Looke, and to morrow late, tell mee,
Whether both the'India's of spice and Myne
    Be where thou leftst them, or lie here with mee.
Aske for those Kings whom thou saw'st yesterday,
And thou shalt heare, All here in one bed lay.

(p. 73)

It is all a trick, of course, an attempt to plunge the world again into darkness and to love. But even while he is saying it, running whatever outlandish sophisms his agile brain admits in order to stay there in bed a little longer, some larger and more important form rises from the depths of consciousness. When it eventually emerges, it is this realization that completely subverts the form of the *alba* and a thousand years of experience of love.

The third stanza begins with a sense of awe and wonder as the speaker realizes fully for the first time what he has been saying all along:

She'is all States, and all Princes, I
    Nothing else is.
Princes doe but play us; compar'd to this,
All honor's mimique; All wealth alchimie.

(p. 73)

In one sense this is merely a summary of the microcosm-macrocosm analogy at the end of the second stanza. But it is more than simply a repetition, for this is no longer a joke, a game, an intellectual ploy to win an argument. It is deadly serious. For if it is true that she is all states or what is best in them contracted and given their essential form—all the richness, splendor, and beauty of the world—if the microcosm-macrocosm analogy, in

15

other words, is really true, then it is also true that nothing else is. The world outside the world of love is unreal. What the speaker has come to realize at this point is a true sense of otherworldliness that completely reverses everything he had ever conceived of before. Otherworldliness, A.O. Lovejoy once wrote, is

> the belief that both the genuinely 'real' and the truly good are radically antithetic in their essential characteristics to anything to be found in man's natural life, in the ordinary course of human experience, however normal, however intelligent, and however fortunate. The world we now and here know—various, mutable, a perpetual flux of states and relations of things, or an ever-shifting phantasmagoria of thoughts and sensations, each of them lapsing into nonentity in the very moment of its birth—seems to the otherworldly mind to have no substance to it.

Nevertheless, Lovejoy continues, most otherworldly philosophies conceive of the possibility of finding in some other world the true reality they seek in shadows here—"some final, fixed, immutable, intrinsic, perfectly satisfactory good, . . . stable, definitive, coherent, self-contained."[9] It is as though the speaker had broken through to himself at last and sensed for the first time that everything he had formerly pursued in his life, everything all men pursue in their lives and spend themselves on, is false: "All honor's mimique; All wealth alchimie." Only this is real. This my honor, this is my wealth. There is no need for me to get out of bed because quite literally there is nothing out there to go to. "Nothing else is." Everything out there is only a shadow of this.

The speaker can then turn to the sun once again in the final section of the poem and address it in a way totally changed from the arrogance and anger at the beginning. The sun is still a super-

16

annuated servant who has certain duties to perform and whose age asks ease. The sun must warm the world, but since the lovers are the only real world, the sun can fulfill its duties in warming them. Therefore, in the image that concludes the poem, breathtaking in its audacity and beauty, the speaker invites the sun to enter the new world of their love:

> Shine here to us, and thou art every where;
> This bed thy center is, these walls, thy spheare.
>
> (p. 73)

But what if the sun did in fact come into the room and revolve in an orbit of the walls? What would happen is the precise image of what the speaker has come to realize about himself and the value to him of his love. The lovers would enter into the artifice of eternity. There would be no alternation of day and night, and therefore no weeks, months, or years, but only, as Donne said in another context, one "first, last, everlasting day," like a constant burning light, an image of his love as well as the speaker's own dazzling consciousness of it.

Almost all of the lyrics in the *Songs and Sonnets* are obsessed with the problem of time and the mutability of human experience. What Donne most often wants to do in his poems is to find some way to fix and make eternal the transient moments within love when flesh and spirit come together and reveal themselves to be one thing. The yearning never failed to fascinate him, and it affords the basis of his most beautiful and most moving poems.

The next work I want to consider deals with this same problem, using many of the same metaphors as in "The Sunne Rising." The title of the poem is "The Anniversarie," and it begins once again with a contrast between the microcosm of the lovers and the macrocosm of the outer world. One is subject to change;

17

the other is changeless. Donne looks first at the outer world and in this case admits its glory and majesty:

> All Kings, and all their favorites,
> All glory'of honors, beauties, wits,
> The Sun it selfe, which makes times, as they passe,
> Is elder by a yeare, now, then it was
> When thou and I first one another saw:
> All other things, to their destruction draw.
>
> (p. 71)

Notice the emphatic use of *all*: *all* Kings, *all* glory, *all* other things. All the glories of the world now move toward their destruction. Even the sun, the measure of time, is caught in its own change. Only this one love remains the same:

> Only our love hath no decay;
> This, no tomorrow hath, nor yesterday,
> Running it never runs from us away,
> But truly keepes his first, last, everlasting day.
>
> (p. 71)

The echo of the lesser doxology that ends the stanza is bold and audacious. The only thing comparable to our love, Donne seems to say, is God himself, who is now and ever shall be, world without end—*per omnia saecula saeculorum*. The phrase skirts the edge of blasphemy, but it is not as shocking as it might otherwise be since it has been prepared for and in part validated by the entire stanza. The lovers are in the world, but not of it. Since their love does not in fact change, it is similar to the timelessness of things in the spiritual world and perhaps even analogous to God himself.

The overall sense of the stanza, then, is curious. Donne attempts to express a common emotion most of us have felt at one time or another in love: that it is the only fixed and permanent thing in a world of change. The stanza is concerned in large part with validating that emotion. But at the same time Donne validates it, he knows it for a solipsistic delusion. These lovers may think their love is eternal, but they too are caught in the flux of things. They too are a year older now than they were when they first met, and they too draw on to their destruction.

This is the point at which the second stanza begins, and Donne introduces it abruptly, with a jolt of paradox:

> Two graves must hide thine and my coarse,
> If one might, death were no divorce.
> Alas, as well as other Princes, wee,
> (Who Prince enough in one another bee,)
> Must leave at last in death, these eyes, and eares,
> Oft fed with true oathes, and with sweet salt teares;
> But soules where nothing dwells but love
> (All other thoughts being inmates) then shall prove
> This, or a love increased there above,
> When bodies to their graves, soules from their graves remove.
>
> (p. 71)

Like all great princes of this world, Donne says, with all the force of the *contemptus mundi* tradition behind him, we too must leave our worldly glory, in this case our bodies and specifically those portals of the body, the eyes and ears, that led us to and into one another. The remainder of the stanza offers some consolation for this loss, in the realization that the soul is immortal and will not only survive the loss of the body, but will prove when it removes from the grave of the flesh what their love truly is. In *The Second Anniversary* Donne speaks of the soul free of the body as having "growen all Ey," not needing to "peepe through lattices of eies, /

19

Nor heare through Laberinths of eares."[10] In the same way he seems to argue here that with our bodies gone we will not need the small openings of eyes and ears. In the simple freedom of the soul alone, we shall be all eye, as though we could see outward simultaneously in all directions at once, from our kneecaps and toes and the small of our back. Since love is soul, we shall step forth then in our true nakedness at last without the old clothes of the body and make love as we never made it before, interpenetrating totally like Milton's angels. What we shall prove is the love we knew on earth, which was soul's love, or else "a love increased there above." I am not entirely certain what that last phrase means because I think it says two things at once. Donne seems to realize in a climactic fashion the fullest completion of love without the body's vestments; but something else, I suspect, flickered in his mind in the middle of that, as though he thought so far and the thought crested, hesitated, and began to turn into its own opposite.

The turning point occurs at the beginning of the final stanza:

And then wee shall be throughly blest,
But wee no more, then all the rest.
(p. 72)

The important word here is *blest*, which glances two ways at once. It refers to the lovers, blessed at last in total fulfillment, but it also refers to the Christian idea of heaven, where the souls of the blessed are subsumed in the love and enjoyment of God. The lovers will be thoroughly blessed, but in such a way that they will lose their individuality and their present love for one another in the spiritual democracy of the Beatific Vision. Love is eternal, Donne implies, but if it becomes too supernatural, it loses its mortal, human nature and in going beyond itself turns into some-

20

thing utterly different. The only proper place for human love is in some curious isthmus of a middle state between the world of becoming and the world of being, for human love partakes of both body and soul in a paradox as strange as the complex nature of man.

In the rest of the stanza, therefore, Donne reverses his direction completely, diving downward to what he now knows is the proper sphere of his love:

> Here upon earth, we'are Kings, and none but wee
> Can be such Kings, nor of such subjects bee;
> Who is so safe as wee? where none can doe
> Treason to us, except one of us two.
> True and false feares let us refraine,
> Let us love nobly,'and live, and adde againe
> Yeares and yeares unto yeares, till we attaine
> To write threescore: this is the second of our raigne.
>
> (p. 72)

Here upon earth these human lovers are uniquely and richly themselves. They are kings, more magnificent than all the other rulers of the earth because of the intimations of another world they find revealed in their love. And since we are kings, Donne says, and since each of us rules the small world of our love and is ruled there, we are perfectly safe. Both of us are true and faithful lovers, and therefore we have no fear that either will betray the other. That is the false fear. The true fear, of course, is death itself, and there is no real solution for that. The poem is simply an affirmation of life hedged in by abnegation and death. For in saying in the last line that "this is the second of our raigne" Donne is speaking not only of the second year of their love, but the endless second of time, the eternal present, the immediate

21

moment that has no successor. The poem ends within a complete awareness of change and death, but at the same time carves out of that awareness a limited sort of human triumph: that one may love nobly and live in such a way that within change, within mortality, one makes here and now in the darkness a fixed, eternal moment of time that "Running . . . never runs from us away, / But truly keepes his first, last, everlasting day."

These, then, or something like them, are the problems the poem explores. It was apparently designed as an anniversary gift at the end of the first year of a love affair or possibly the first year of Donne's marriage to Anne More. What I would like to do now is to suggest what may have another point of origin for the poem. For the term *anniversary* was used very differently in the Renaissance from the way we use it today. We tend to associate it almost exclusively with marriage. In the Renaissance it was associated most often with death. The term was first used in an ecclesiastical sense, summarized by Thomas Blount in the seventeenth century: "Anniversary days were of old those days, wherein the Martyrdoms or Deaths of Saints were celebrated yearly in the Church; or the days whereon, at every years end, Men were wont to pray for the Souls of their deceased Friends, according to the continual Custom of Roman Catholicks" (*OED*, "Anniversary," *adj*. 1). The word *anniversary* was also used to refer to "the mass or religious service in memory of someone on the day of his death, also called 'year's mind'" (*OED, sb*. 2). The term also referred to the "*annuale*, or commemorative service performed daily for a year after the death of a person" (*OED, sb*. 3). Moreover, there was a specific kind of poem in the Renaissance known as an *anniversary*. Donne himself wrote two of them on the death of Elizabeth Drury, which Professor Martz will talk about this evening. In entitling these poems *The Anniversaries* Donne referred not only to the fact that he was commemorating the anniversary of Elizabeth Drury's death. He also referred to the fact that he was writing a specific kind of elegy. Julius Caesar Scaliger in his *Poetices Libri Septem*, published in the mid-sixteenth century, describes the anniversary as a variety of epitaph. An epitaph, Scaliger explains, was a poem recited over the grave and either left there as an offering or else inscribed on a stone tablet and affixed to the tomb.[11] Renaissance epitaphs tended to be very long and very elaborate. George Puttenham, for example, spoke of them as the tedious product of bastard rimers "to be hanged up in Churches and chauncells ouer the tombes of great men and others, which be so exceeding long as one must haue halfe a dayes leasure to read one of them & must be called away before he come halfe to the end, or else be locked into the Church by the Sexten as I my selfe was once serued reading an Epitaph in a certain cathedrall Church of England."[12] Such an epitaph, recited over the grave as part of the funeral service, was known as the *epitaphium recens*, or *immediate epitaph*. A variant of this was also used to commemorate the dead at certain fixed intervals of time, either monthly, known as "monethes mindes,"[13] or yearly, on the anniversary of the death. The poetic form for such a yearly remembrance was known as the *epitaphium anniversarium* or *anniversary epitaph* and was regarded as having certain classical models. Scaliger mentions an anniversary by Pericles recited at Athens and recorded by Thucydides. He also mentions one by Plato and three others by Aristides.[14] The form was widely known in the Renaissance. In *Much Ado About Nothing* Shakespeare has Claudio come at night to the tomb of Hero, who is supposed to have just died. He recites a poem in her memory, entitled *Epitaph*, and hangs the scroll on the tomb as an offering. This is what Scaliger would call the *epitaphium recens*. Claudio then

23

promises to commemorate the death in the future by using the form of the *epitaphium anniversarium*: "Now," he says, "unto thy bones good night! / Yearly will I do this rite."[15] The *Epitaph* Claudio recites follows the rigorous format prescribed for such poems in Renaissance manuals of poetics. Scaliger, for example, says that an epitaph should have five parts: (1) praise, (2) demonstration of loss, (3) grief, (4) consolation, and (5) exhortation. In an anniversary all these parts are present except grief, for "no one," Scaliger says, "can mourn the dead for as long as a year or more, not to mention the fact that often so much time has passed that neither the fathers, nor their children, nor their children's children are still alive."[16]

This, then, is the information. Perhaps by being aware of it, we can rub some of the tarnish of time off Donne's poem and make it shine as bright for us as it did when it was new. What I am about to suggest in no way contradicts the essential nature of the poem as an anniversary celebration of a year and lifetime of love. It simply restores an additional dimension of meaning lost to us through the passage of time.

Donne's poem is a celebration of life that confronts change, age, and death and achieves a very human, very limited, but very real triumph, like a torch consuming itself in darkness. Suppose, in writing the poem, Donne hit upon the idea of taking the form of the *epitaphium anniversarium* and, turning it upside-down, used it to celebrate not death, but life, as the ambiguity of the term *anniversary* as used in the Renaissance would allow him to do. The poem would then become an even stronger affirmation and celebration of life, for the reversal of the form, making a love poem out of a funeral poem, and the total shift in emphasis thereby would itself be a reenactment of the very thing Donne is talking about in the poem. Instead of memorializing life swallowed up in death, we would have life flaming in the darkness that surrounds it, just as the poem flames in the darkness of its form.

The second suggestion I would like to make is that after having decided to reverse the form in this way, Donne then had a model or outline to follow in the remainder of the poem; for the anniversary, remember, was regarded as having a fixed, progressive structure and certain fixed parts. First was the act of praise. This would in the hypothesis correspond to the first stanza, the praise of all the splendor of this world, moving toward destruction, and especially the lovers, who keep their "first, last, everlasting day." The second part of the anniversary is the demonstration of loss. This would correspond to the beginning of the second stanza, where the loss demonstrated is the loss of the body through death, the eyes and ears and various senses that brought the lovers together. The third part of the anniversary is the consolation. The usual consolation in the Christian tradition is the realization that our souls survive after death and find essential happiness in a world beyond the grave. Toward the end of the second stanza and the beginning of the third Donne proceeds into this standard consolation, but he ends up with something else instead. The lovers' souls will survive after death and either find a fuller expression of love without bodies, or else they will be subsumed in a greater love for God. Either way they will lose the rich, human love they enjoy here on earth. With this thought in mind Donne arrives at the final part of the anniversary, the exhortation, in which the living are urged to emulate in their lives the great deeds and virtues of the one who is dead. Donne's exhortation is addressed to the lovers themselves who, in this curious reversal of the form, are the same ones whose death is being lamented:

Let us love nobly,'and live, and adde againe

Yeares and yeares unto yeares, till we attaine

To write threescore: this is the second of our raigne.

(p. 72)

The human love they enjoy here, we learn from the totality of the poem, is similar to the supernatural essence of love in God. Hence the flashes of unearthly beauty and peace they perceive. By living a life of love, therefore, they can enjoy it now for the human thing it is, combining both physical and spiritual, body and soul. They can also be assured that after death their love will survive in some fashion forever. That is the exhortation and the final consolation of the poem, which is very worldly, I think, very Christian, and very true.

*Ed. note: The professor is George P. Hayes, chairman of the department of English at Agnes Scott College, 1927-1965, and member of the department faculty until his retirement in 1967.

Notes:

[1]John Donne, *The Elegies and The Songs and Sonnets*, ed. Helen Gardner (Oxford: The Clarendon Press, 1965), p. 90. All subsequent quotations from the *Songs and Sonnets* are taken from this edition.

[2]*Odes*, I, xi.

[3]"To his Coy Mistress," *The Poems and Letters of Andrew Marvell*, ed. H.M. Margoliouth (Oxford: The Clarendon Press, 1952), I, 26.

[4]Cf. *Amores*, I, xiii.

[5]Alfred Jeanroy, *La Poesie Lyrique des Troubadours* (Paris: Henri Didier, 1934), II, 294.

[6]*Romeo and Juliet*, III, v, 1-3, 6-11. Cf. also *Troilus and Cressida*, IV, ii, 1-18.

[7]*After Experience* (New York: Harper and Row, 1968), p. 18.

[8]*Collected Poems* (London: Chatto and Windus, 1956), p. 48.

[9]*The Great Chain of Being* (New York: Harper and Brothers, 1960), pp. 25-26.

[10]John Donne, *The Anniversaries*, ed. Frank Manley (Baltimore: The Johns Hopkins Press, 1963), pp. 97, 100.

[11]*Poetices Libri Septem* (Stuttgart-Bad Cannstatt: Friedrich Frommann Verlag, 1964). p. 168.

[12]*The Arte of English Poesie*, ed. G.D. Willcock and A. Walker (Cambridge: Cambridge University Press, 1936), p. 48.

[13]Puttenham, *loc. cit.*

[14]*Poetices, loc. cit.*

[15]*Much Ado about Nothing*, V, iii, 22-23.

[16]*Poetices, loc. cit.*: "In recenti partes hae: Laudes, Iacturae demonstratio, Luctus, Consolatio, Exhortatio. In Anniuersario hae eadem omnia praeter luctum. Nemo enim iam annum bienniùmue defunctum deflet. Multo verò minus si tantum temporis exactum sit, vt neque patres, neque liberi illius illorúmue sint superstites."

Louis L. Martz

DONNE'S *ANNIVERSARIES* REVISITED

On the four-hundredth anniversary of the birth of John Donne it seems appropriate to talk about two poems that he called *Anniversaries*. But my title implies a small private anniversary which I view with a mixture of surprise and dismay: it was twenty-five years ago that I published an essay on these poems—an essay that has provoked, or evoked, a flood of corrections, rebukes, or (occasionally) sympathetic extensions. I do not mean to take sole responsibility for this scholarly and critical controversy. It would have happened anyhow, for in 1950 Marjorie Nicolson, working independently, published an equally controversial essay on the *Anniversaries* which has provoked an equal number of corrections and rejoinders.

Now I believe that the usual run for any scholarly or critical point of view is not likely to be much more than twenty-five years. By that time a new generation has effected so drastic a change in approach to any given literary work that the twenty-five-year-old essay or book has begun to seem antiquated. I should like, therefore, to attempt a correction of a point of view set forth long ago.

The process of correction began with a moment still vivid to me. It occurred at a meeting of the Modern Language Association in 1956, when a young man, then a graduate student at Harvard, came up to me and said, "I'm glad to meet you—I've just published an essay attacking your faulty account of Donne's *First*

29

Anniversary. Could I send you a copy of it?" Naturally I was delighted to hear of this attack, and when I came to read Ralph Maud's essay I found it presented with such tact and courtesy that I underwent a gradual conversion toward his point of view. My old essay treated the *First Anniversary* as an effort at formal religious meditation, and thus regarded the poem as a failure, since it did not succeed in developing the image of the dead girl, Elizabeth Drury, into a symbol of religious virtue that would unify the poem and answer the goals of meditation. But Maud pointed out that it was possible to take another view: to see the work as a *didactic* poem, designed to teach contempt of the world. From this standpoint, Maud argued, one can see "how the structure and thought" of the work "go together and produce a coherent poem."[1]

This process of gradual correction has proceeded with the help of at least a dozen first-rate essays over the past fifteen years, along with Frank Manley's important edition of 1963. Indeed the process has gone on to the very latest moment, for just as I finished writing this lecture, a magazine arrived in my mailbox with the very latest (December, 1971) account of the *Anniversaries*. Ruth Fox, in this essay, has given a point of view with which I wholly agree: that the poems present "the celebration of goodness in the soul of men," and that "the end of the processes of anatomy and progress should lie in the soul's knowledge of self as self and not as mere 'in-mate soule.' "[2]

But why, we must ask, have these poems so gripped the imagination of the past quarter-century? Why, after nearly three centuries of neglect, since Dryden's "Eleonora," have they come to appear as two of the greatest poems in the greatest era of English literature? The poems are, we should remember, almost exactly contemporary with *King Lear* and *The Tempest*, and in their own way deal with the basic issues found in those plays: the dissolution of order in the world, and the creation of a new order within the self.[3] In this theme, I believe, we may find the basic cause of the poems' appeal: for Donne now seems to speak directly to us, explaining what it is to live in a world that seems to be dying in the throes of some mysterious renewal.

But there are other, less essential, ways in which the *Anniversaries* hold a special appeal. As literary scholars, we love the poems because they coalesce and focus all the warring elements in Donne's violent and dazzling career. The strong satiric passages in the *Anniversaries* recall for us Donne's early satires and satirical love-elegies, especially Satire III, with its denunciation of the world, the flesh, and the devil:

> Know thy foes: The foule Devill, whom thou
> Striv'st to please, for hate, not love, would allow
> Thee faine, his whole Realme to be quit; and as
> The worlds all parts wither away and passe,
> So the worlds selfe, thy other lov'd foe, is
> In her decrepit wayne, and thou loving this,
> Dost love a wither'd and worne strumpet; last,
> Flesh (it selfes death) and joyes which flesh can taste,
> Thou lov'st; and thy faire goodly soule, which doth
> Give this flesh power to taste joy, thou dost loath.
>   Seeke true religion. O where?[4]
>
>   (33-43)

Meanwhile the strong religious themes of the *Anniversaries* evoke Donne's *Holy Sonnets*, which carry on his search for true religion by the process of religious meditation, answering that cry, "O where?" by pointing toward the heart of man:

31

What if this present were the worlds last night?
Marke in my heart, O Soule, where thou dost dwell,
The picture of Christ crucified, and tell
Whether that countenance can thee affright . . . .[5]

Thirdly, in their didactic moments, the *Anniversaries* foretell
Donne's later career as the most brilliant preacher of his age,
preaching "like an Angel from a cloud," as Izaak Walton reports,
"but in none."[6] This moving combination of clarity and eloquence
in Donne's sermons can be seen from a beautiful passage that
Frank Manley properly associates with the opening lines of the
First Anniversary:

> *Primus actus voluntatis est Amor*: Philosophers and Divines
> agree in that, That the will of man cannot be idle, and the
> first act that the will of man produces, is Love; for till it love
> something, prefer and chuse something, till it would have
> something, it is not a will; neither can it turn upon any ob-
> ject, before God. So that this first, and general, and natural
> love of God, is not begotten in my soul, nor produced by my
> soul, but created and infus'd with my soul, and as my soul;
> there is no soul that knows she is a soul, without such a
> general sense of the love of God.[7]

These then are the motifs, satire, meditation, and sermon,
out of which Donne's *Anniversaries* are composed. Indeed these
poems are the axis upon which Donne's outward career shifts
from secular to sacred. I say, outward career, because within,
Donne's sensibility remained from youth to age a turbulent mixture of unruly elements, which the oscillating structure of the
Anniversaries may serve to represent and to control, after the
manner suggested by the great passage in Satire III:

32

On a huge hill,
Cragged, and steep, Truth stands, and hee that will
Reach her, about must, and about must goe . . . .
(79-81)

At the same time the poems sum up and focus the varied and conflicting currents of Renaissance culture up to the year 1612. The satiric aspects remind us of the Renaissance interest in classical Roman satire.[8] The eulogies of the dead girl remind us of Petrarch's Laura and her enormous heritage of praise down through the centuries since Petrarch sang his "long deceased woes" (as Philip Sidney put it in the fifteenth sonnet of *Astrophel and Stella*). Meanwhile the religious aspects, with their overtones of devotion to a "blessed maid," reflect many centuries of medieval devotion, while other aspects of the poem recall the medieval literature of contempt of the world, along with the legend of Astraea and the ancient tradition of Wisdom.[9] At the same time the poems contain the meditative structures of the late Middle Ages and the Counter-Reformation, along with the trinitarian doctrine of St. Augustine and St. Bernard. These are poems that stand at the watershed between ancient and modern; they seem to pronounce a valediction or an elegy upon the Renaissance quest for an ideal harmony of body and spirit. They hold the past in memory, while the speaker's understanding and will move toward the future.

-2-

The title-page of the *First Anniversary* provides the clue to its basic, controlling image and method: "An Anatomy of the World. Wherein, by Occasion of the untimely death of Mistris Elizabeth Drury the frailty and the decay of this whole world is

33

represented." And the introductory part of the poem clarifies the point:

> But though it be too late to succour thee,
> Sicke world, yea dead, yea putrified, since shee
> Thy'ntrinsique Balme, and thy preservative,
> Can never be renew'd, thou never live,
> I (since no man can make thee live) will trie,
> What we may gaine by thy Anatomy.
> Her death hath taught us dearely, that thou art
> Corrupt and mortall in thy purest part.
> Let no man say, the world it selfe being dead,
> 'Tis labour lost to have discovered
> The worlds infirmities, since there is none
> Alive to study this dissectione . . . .[10]
>
> (55-66)

This principle of dissection forms the very method of the poem, as several critics have seen. The poem, says Maud, "is an 'anatomy,' a demonstration of parts"; and Manley, noting that the poem's tone is "analytic and satirical," says that it proceeds "from part to part in rigid logical sequence . . . . Its ultimate discovery is a universe of death."[11]

It is widely (though not completely) accepted now that the *Anatomy* falls into seven carefully dissected parts (the medical overtone seems appropriate), as follows: a long introduction, defining the didactic purpose of the dissection, then five main sections that analyze the body of the work, followed by a brief conclusion. At the same time each of the five main sections is precisely sub-divided into three parts:[12]

(1)   a meditation, "shot through with satire,"[13] on some aspect of the world's frailty and decay;

34

(2)   a shorter sub-section, a eulogy, praising the dead girl in elaborate hyperbole as the essence of virtue, and thus relating the poem to the ancient genre of funeral praise, as O.B. Hardison has shown;

(3)   a brief concluding section, marked off by a refrain, "Shee, shee is dead; shee's dead," a section which might be called a "moral," or "moral exhortation."

Each meditation tends to have its own internal consistency, working up to a climax that forces a strong pause before the poem shifts to the eulogy. Thus the first section begins with the fall of man, and the meditation on mankind's decay works toward a climax at line 161:

> Thus man, this worlds Vice-Emperor, in whom
> All faculties, all graces are at home;
> And if in other Creatures they appeare,
> They're but mans ministers, and Legats there,
> To worke on their rebellions, and reduce
> Them to Civility, and to mans use.
> This man, whom God did wooe, and loth t'attend
> Till man came up, did downe to man descend,
> This man, so great, that all that is, is his,
> Oh what a trifle, and poore thing he is!
>   (161-70)

Then, shifting to the eulogy, we begin a movement that reaches its own climax in the refrain:

> If man were any thing, he's nothing now:
> Helpe, or at least some time to wast, allow
> T'his other wants, yet when he did depart
> With her, whom we lament, he lost his hart.

35

> She, of whom th'Auncients seem'd to prophesie,
> When they call'd vertues by the name of shee,
> She in whom vertue was so much refin'd,
> That for Allay unto so pure a minde
> Shee tooke the weaker Sex, she that could drive
> The poysonous tincture, and the stayne of *Eve*,
> Out of her thoughts, and deeds; and purifie
> All, by a true religious Alchimy;
> Shee, shee is dead; shee's dead . . . .
>
> (171-83)

And finally, the moral exhortation, following from the refrain, serves to tie the two preceding parts together:

> Shee, shee is dead; shee's dead: when thou knowest this,
> Thou knowest how poore a trifling thing man is.
> And learn'st thus much by our Anatomee,
> The heart being perish'd, no part can be free.
> And that except thou feed (not banquet) on
> The supernaturall food, Religion,
> Thy better Grouth growes withered, and scant;
> Be more then man, or thou'rt lesse then an Ant.
>
> (183-90)

Thus the five main sections of the *Anatomy* tend to fall not so much into three parts, as into two contrasting parts, one negative, one positive, both being pulled together by this brief exhortation which drives home didactically the meaning of the contrast.

Now if we stand back to look at the whole *Anatomy*, it soon becomes clear that the satirical texture is dominating the poem, as a brief set of statistics for the main sections will indicate:

I.   80 lines of satire: 12 of praise.

II.   28 lines of satire: 18 of praise.
III. 62 lines of satire: 16 of praise.
IV.   20 lines of satire: 10 of praise.

Then in section V something astonishing happens: the mode of satire invades and overthrows the eulogy at line 415, with the result that the climax of this eulogy becomes a bitter denunciation of the world:

> She from whose influence all Impressions came,
> But, by Receivers impotencies, lame,
> Who, though she could not transubstantiate
> All states to gold, yet guilded every state,
> So that some Princes have some temperance;
> Some Counsaylors some purpose to advance
> The common profite; and some people have
> Some stay, no more then Kings should give, to crave;
> Some women have some taciturnity;
> Some Nunneries, some graines of chastity.
> She that did thus much, and much more could doe,
> But that our age was Iron, and rusty too,
> Shee, shee is dead; shee's dead: when thou knowst this,
> Thou knowest how drie a Cinder this world is.
>
> (415-28)

Thus the power of the eulogy is destroyed by the power of satiric denunciation; the image of virtue is powerless to control the world's corruption, powerless to avert the direction of the poem toward the grave. That is why I felt, twenty-five years ago, that the eulogies had failed to perform their part effectively, and that the poem therefore failed, despite some brilliant parts. And the poem does fail to reach the goal of religious meditation, which should be found in a resolution of the soul's problems, through a

37

sense of devotion to God. But I see now that a failure in meditation may become a success in poetry.[14] That is, the poem successfully enacts a failure in the meditative process: it uses the forms of meditation, in its five-fold, three-fold (or two-fold) structure, but it uses that structure for denunciation, not for devotion. The *Anatomy* is a powerfully successful satire; it is not, at heart, a meditation, for it deals with a world in which the heart has died.[15] That final invasion of the eulogy by satire marks the death of virtue's power in this world, and so the poem ends with the loathsome image of the corpse being dissected:

> But as in cutting up a man that's dead,
> The body will not last out to have read
> On every part, and therefore men direct
> Their speech to parts, that are of most effect;
> So the worlds carcasse would not last, if I
> Were punctuall in this Anatomy.
> Nor smels it well to hearers, if one tell
> Them their disease, who faine would think they're wel.
> Here therefore be the end . . . .
>
> (435-43)

And it is the end, except for thirty lines of epilogue in which Donne makes clear his posture as a public speaker: an orator, a prophet, a teacher of anatomy.

Thus the poem's sharp and precise division into parts, which I once saw as a flaw, now seems quite in accord with the central image of the dissection, the anatomy. In this "demonstration of parts" the world is appropriately cut up into these clear divisions and subdivisions, in order that we may see clearly the corruption in all those parts.

But what then is the role of the worthy "Shee," the idealized figure of the girl, in a poem which Ben Jonson thought "was profane and full of blasphemies" because he evidently saw that the imagery surrounding the dead girl held suggestions of saint-hood, divinity, the Virgin Mary, even something of the Logos or of Christ himself? Donne's answer to Jonson remains still the steady light: "to which he answered that he described the Idea of a Woman and not as she was."[16] Aside from his title-page, and the introductory poem by Joseph Hall, Donne has made every possible effort to keep the figure of the actual young girl out of our minds. Her name never occurs within the poem: it is always that "Soule" or that "Shee" which is both woman and soul. From the opening lines of the *Anatomy* this is true:

> When that rich soule which to her Heaven is gone,
> Whom all they celebrate, who know they have one,
> (For who is sure he hath a soule, unlesse
> It see, and Judge, and follow worthinesse,
> And by Deedes praise it? He who doth not this,
> May lodge an In-mate soule, but tis not his.)
>
> (1-6)

By the three-fold action of seeing, judging, and following "worthi-nesse" we may be able to discover the reality of our own souls.

Then Donne turns to the ancient figure of speech that says the world is dead or stunned by her death—a conceit based on a feeling that we all may share in moments of immense grief, a sense that the world is empty, that we cannot go on living. And along with this image Donne now introduces a very strange and interesting distinction:

> Some moneths she hath beene dead (but being dead,
> Measures of times are all determined)

39

But long shee'ath beene away, long, long, yet none
Offers to tell us who it is that's gone.

(39-42)

Is this Donne's way of telling us that the poem is not of course
simply about a dead girl, but is really about the loss of the quali-
ties that this young and innocent being may be taken to represent: youth, beauty, purity, virtue, religion?[17] "Who it is that's
gone" is something that has long been away, long, long, ever since
the fall of man, ever since the fall of the angels.

The symbol of "Shee," then, becomes the image of ancient
virtue struggling vainly for life in a twilight world of decay. Thus
every one of the five main sections must repeat its strict rhythm
of contrast: satirical meditation, praise and lament for the lost
heart of virtue, and the exhortation: give up this rotten world.
There can be no progress, no redemption, in such a dissected
structure: the *Anatomy* suggests a mind caught in a deadly oscil-
lation, caught in a narrowing gyre that ends in the grave. There
is a dramatic flagging of energy as the poem concludes, as though
the speaker has worn himself out by his tirade and has given up,
exhausted by a sense of nullity: "Here therefore be the end."

-3-

But there is another *Anniversary*, with a different title page:
"The Second Anniversarie. Of the Progres of the Soule. Wherein:
By Occasion of the Religious Death of Mistris Elizabeth Drury,
the incommodities of the Soule in this life and her exaltation in
the next, are Contemplated." As several commentators have
pointed out, the word "contemplated" suggests a mental process
quite different from that suggested by the word "represented" in
the title of the *Anatomy*. It is the difference between inward self-

40

consciousness and external demonstration. Yet we must note how closely the two poems are tied together. The *Second Anniversary* begins where the *First Anniversary* has ended: with the image of a corpse, even more gruesome than the implied cadaver at the end of the *Anatomy*:

> Or as sometimes in a beheaded man,
> Though at those two Red seas, which freely ran,
> One from the Trunke, another from the Head,
> His soule be saild, to her eternall bed,
> His eies will twinckle, and his tongue will roll,
> As though he beckned, and cal'd backe his Soul,
> He graspes his hands, and he puls up his feet,
> And seemes to reach, and to step forth to meet
> His soule; when all these motions which we saw,
> Are but as Ice, which crackles at a thaw:
> Or as a Lute, which in moist weather, rings
> Her knell alone, by cracking at her strings.
> So strugles this dead world, now shee is gone;
> For there is motion in corruption.
>
> (9-22)

In this state of corruption, the speaker now finds hope within a certain "motion," an action that will fix the mind upon the image of virtue, while waiting out the time until death or dooms-day bring release:

> Thirst for that time, O my insatiate soule,
> And serve thy thirst, with Gods safe-sealing Bowle.
>
> (45-46)

In accord with this "motion" we note that the speaker has shifted from the stance of the didactic speaker toward a mode of self-

41

address, the essential mode of the meditative action. And in accord with this action the structure of the *Second Anniversary* undergoes a gradual modulation, after a reminiscence of the *Anatomy's* three-fold construction within the first two sections. This change can best be demonstrated by an outline that represents a significant extension from the outline offered in my original essay:[18]

Introduction, 1-44.
Section I, 45-84.
   1. Meditation, 45-64: "A just disestimation of this world."
   2. Eulogy, 65-80.
   3. Refrain and Moral, 81-84.
Section II, 85-156.
   1. Meditation, 85-120: "Contemplation of our state in our death-bed."
   2. Eulogy, 121-46.
   3. Moral, 147-56.
Section III, 157-250.
   1. Meditation.
      a. 157-78: "Incommodities of the Soule in the Body."
      b. 179-219: the soul's "liberty by death."
   2. Eulogy (with brief moral), 220-50.
Section IV, 251-320.
   1. Meditation.
      a. 251-89: the soul's "ignorance in this life."
      b. 290-300: the soul's "knowledge in the next" life.
   2. Eulogy (with brief moral), 301-20.
Section V, 321-82.
   1. Meditation.

a. 321-38: "Of our company in this life."

b. 339-55: of our company "in the next" life.

2. Eulogy (with brief moral), 356-82.

Section VI, 383-470.

1. Meditation.

a. 383-434: "Of essentiall joy in this life."

b. 435-46: of essential joy "in the next" life.

2. Eulogy, 447-70.

Section VII, 471-510.

1. Meditation.

a. 471-86: of "accidentall joyes" in this life.

b. 487-96: of "accidentall joyes" in the next
life.

2. Eulogy, 497-510.

Conclusion, 511-28.

As this outline indicates, the third section of the poem (out of the seven main sections) begins to show a development that is never found in the *Anatomy*. For Section III, while retaining some echoes of the satirical meditation, eulogy, and moral, has developed a basically different structure by dividing the meditation into two parts, giving up the refrain, and cutting down the moral to only four lines. I dimly glimpsed this point in my earlier essay, but I did not see the meaning of this shift in structure until Frank Manley suggested that the three-fold divisions of the *Anatomy* resembled the three-fold division of the powers of the soul, Memory, Understanding, and Will: the interior Trinity which meditation strives to integrate.[19] That effort at integration does not succeed in the *Anatomy*, because the satiric impulse wins out. But, if we look closely at Section III of the *Progress*, we notice that it falls into three well-proportioned parts: a mathematical proportion of 2:4:3.

First, we have a section of twenty-two lines (157-78) which gives the memory of the inevitably sinful birth of the soul in the flesh (equivalent to the satirical meditation in the *Anatomy*):

> Thinke but how poore thou wast, how obnoxious,
> Whom a small lump of flesh could poison thus.
> This curded milke, this poore unlittered whelpe
> My body, could, beyond escape, or helpe,
> Infect thee with originall sinne, and thou
> Couldst neither then refuse, nor leave it now.
>
> (163-68)

But at line 179 a new development begins, a section of forty-one lines which conveys an understanding of the soul's true liberty:

> But thinke that Death hath now enfranchis'd thee,
> Thou hast thy'expansion now and libertee;
> Thinke that a rusty Peece, discharg'd, is flowen
> In peeces, and the bullet is his owne,
> And freely flies: This to thy soule allow,
> Thinke thy sheell broke, thinke thy Soule hatch'd but now.
>
> (179-84)

And then follows the splendid imagination of the soul's movement through the spheres toward a discovery of its true unity of being, toward a knowledge of man's true destiny and original excellence:

> And as these stars were but so many beades
> Strunge on one string, speed undistinguish'd leades
> Her through those spheares, as through the beades, a string,
> Whose quicke succession makes it still one thing:
> As doth the Pith, which, least our Bodies slacke,

44

Strings fast the little bones of necke, and backe;
So by the soule doth death string Heaven and Earth,
For when our soule enjoyes this her third birth,
(Creation gave her one, a second, grace,)
Heaven is as neare, and present to her face,
As colours are, and objects, in a roome
Where darknesse was before, when Tapers come.
This must, my soule, thy long-short Progresse bee . . . .
                    (207-19)

And now, at line 220, begins a section of thirty-one lines, a eulogy in which the emotions of the will (love and wonder) are moved by the vision of perfect virtue:

                    we understood
Her by her sight, her pure and eloquent blood
Spoke in her cheekes, and so distinckly wrought,
That one might almost say, her bodie thought,
Shee, shee, thus richly, and largely hous'd, is gone:
And chides us slow-pac'd snailes, who crawle upon
Our prisons prison, earth, nor thinke us well
Longer, then whil'st we beare our brittle shell.
                    (243-50)

The slight vestige of the refrain ties this poem, by contrast, to the *Anatomy*, while the imagery of the "shell" ties together the second and third sub-sections of this part.

The same three-fold movement can be seen in each of the remaining sections of the *Progress*, a meditative action fully in accord with the practice of the powers of the soul as outlined, for example, in Edward Dawson's treatise of 1614:

. . . we must begin the first pointe of our Meditation, exercis-

ing thereon the three powers of our soule, Memorie, Understanding, and Will. With our memorie we must (as it were)
rehearse unto our selves in order, that which is conteined in
the first point of the matter we prepared, calling to mind also
such things as we have read in the holy Scripture, and other
good Authors, or heard of discreet and devout persons, yf it
make for the matter we have in hand; and lay open to the
view of our understanding the persons, wordes, and workes
contained in the first point, if it containe any, if none, at least
the most notable matters therin.

Then we must exercise our understanding upon that
which the memory hath proposed, and search out diligently,
what may be considered about that present object, inferring
one thing from another, framing from thence true, pious, and
spirituall conceipts, fit to move our Will to vertuous affections. Lastly for that the will is naturally inclined and moved
to affect those things which the understanding proposeth, we
must procure with all diligence to stir up in our selves those
affections which the operations of our understanding going
before, incline us unto.

And having thus exercised the three powers of our soule
upon the first point, we must passe on to the next.[20]

We are watching the progress of the restoration of the three-
fold Image of God within man, in accordance with the theology
set forth by St. Augustine in his great treatise on the Trinity and
after him by St. Bernard. As the soul moves its three powers over
each point, the idealized girl gradually becomes a symbol of that
interior Image. And so the mind of the speaker, emerging from
the grave of the *Anatomy*, draws imperfectly, but certainly, toward the renewal of that Image. It is a process that we see, best

of all, in the sixth section of the poem, which opens with a poignant memory of the world set forth by Donne in his *Songs and Sonnets*:

> Dost thou love
> Beauty? (And Beauty worthyest is to move)
> Poore couse'ned cose'nor, that she, and that thou,
> Which did begin to love, are neither now.
> You are both fluid, chang'd since yesterday;
> Next day repaires, (but ill) last daies decay.
> Nor are, (Although the river keep the name)
> Yesterdaies waters, and to daies the same.
> So flowes her face, and thine eies, neither now
> That saint, nor Pilgrime, which your loving vow
> Concernd, remaines; but whil'st you thinke you bee
> Constant, you'are howrely in inconstancee.
>
> (389-400)

With that sad, yet accepting look backward at the mutable world of earthly lovers, the speaker's mind turns gradually toward the Image of divine love:

> Shee, who had Here so much essentiall joye,
> As no chance could distract, much lesse destroy;
> Who with Gods presence was acquainted so,
> (Hearing, and speaking to him) as to know
> His face, in any naturall Stone, or Tree,
> Better then when in Images they bee:
> Who kept, by diligent devotion,
> Gods Image, in such reparation,
> Within her heart, that what decay was growen,
> Was her first Parents fault, and not her own:

Who being solicited to any Act,
Still heard God pleading his safe precontract;
Who by a faithfull confidence, was here
Betrothed to God, and now is married there,
Whose twilights were more cleare, then our mid day,
Who dreamt devoutlier, then most use to pray;
Who being heare fild with grace, yet strove to bee,
Both where more grace, and more capacitee
At once is given: shee to Heaven is gone,
Who made this world in some proportion
A heaven, and here, became unto us all,
Joye, (as our joyes admit) essentiall.

(449-70)

Here, then, is the culmination and resolution of both *Anniversaries*. They are companion-poems, as Miss Nicolson has said,[21] like "L'Allegro" and "Il Penseroso," although the *Anatomy* is hardly in the mode of *Allegro*: one would rather call it *L'Amaro*, the bitter one. Yet the analogy will hold to this extent: neither *Anniversary* can be read successfully without the presence of the other. Both *Anniversaries* form a double poem in which the sadness of untimely death is converted to the consolation of a religious death, while the speaker himself is transformed from the bitter, angry voice of the public satirist into the gentler, inward voice of one who has learned how to see, and judge, and follow worthiness. In this double poem, as the speaker says at the very close of the *Progress*, he has sought to praise that worthiness by the deed of poetry:

Since his will is, that to posteritee,
Thou shouldest for life, and death, a patterne bee,
And that the world should notice have of this,

The purpose, and th'Autority is his;

Thou art the Proclamation; and I ame

The Trumpet, at whose voice the people came.

Notes:

¹Maud, p. 225. For full references to books and articles see the Bibliography at the
end of this lecture.

²Fox, pp. 538, 541.

³Cf. Patrick Cruttwell's essay on the relation between the *Anniversaries* and Shakespeare's last plays.

⁴Text of Satire III is quoted from *John Donne: The Satires, Epigrams and Verse
Letters*, ed. W. Milgate (Oxford: The Clarendon Press, 1967), pp. 10-14.

⁵Text is quoted from *John Donne: The Divine Poems*, ed. Helen Gardner (Oxford: The
Clarendon Press, 1952), p. 10.

⁶Izaak Walton, *Lives*, World's Classics edn. (London: Oxford University Press, 1927),
p. 49.

⁷*The Sermons of John Donne*, ed. G. R. Potter and Evelyn M. Simpson, 10 vols.
(Berkeley: University of California Press, 1953-61), VI, 361. See Manley, p. 42.

⁸Also "Menippean satire," as Northrop Frye has suggested: *Anatomy of Criticism*
(Princeton: Princeton University Press, 1957), pp. 298, 308-12.

⁹See Nicolson, pp. 74-9 (1950 edn.); Manley, pp. 20-40.

¹⁰Quotations from the *Anniversaries* are taken from Manley's edition, with the use of
i, j, u, and v modernized.

¹¹Maud, p. 218; Manley, p. 48.

¹²See the detailed outline of the *First Anniversary* in my book *The Poetry of
Meditation*, pp. 221-23. After studying carefully the various modifications in this outline
that other readers have suggested (see, for example, Hardison, pp. 176-77) I still hold to
my original view in this case.

¹³Manley, p. 45.

¹⁴Cf. Carol Sicherman, pp. 128-29: "Considered as an effort to reach intellectual
clarity concerning this world and his place in that world, the poem fails . . . yet whatever
the poet-speaker's original idea of success may have been, the poem succeeds artistically,
in two ways. First, as a separate poem it succeeds simply as an eloquent expression of the
anguished discovery of failure. Second, as half of a diptych, its culminating discovery
enables its sequel to attain a better balance of intellect and emotion, to attain the ultimate
insights which unify the entire bipartite poem."

¹⁵Cf. Harold Love, pp. 127, 129: "Elizabeth Drury exists in the poem not only as the
soul of the world whose withdrawal from it has caused its corruption but as the heart of
the world, a heart that despite its perfections has been finally unable to avoid becoming
involved in the universal process of corruption that began with the fall." "If the purest
part is rotten, there can be no hope of soundness anywhere."

¹⁶"Conversations with Drummond," *Ben Jonson*, ed. C.H. Herford, Percy and Evelyn
Simpson, 11 vols. (Oxford: The Clarendon Press, 1925-52), I, 133 (modernized).

[17]Cf. Nicolson, p. 70 (1950 edn.); Williamson, *Milton and Others*, p. 159.

[18]The following outline was first presented in the Commentary for *The Anchor Anthology of Seventeenth-Century Verse*, vol. I, ed. Martz (Garden City, N.Y.: Doubleday, 1969); reprinted in The Norton Library Series under the title *English Seventeenth-Century Verse* (New York: Norton, 1973), pp. 475-76. The quotations in the outline are taken from the marginal notes in the 1612 edition of the *Second Anniversary*.

[19]See Manley, pp. 41-3. In *The Poetry of Meditation* (1954), pp. 34-6, I discussed the meaning of this three-fold action of the powers of the soul, with reference to St. Bernard and St. Bonaventure; in the revised edition of 1962, responding to a plea by my friend John Smith, I noted (p. xxiv) the primary source for this theory of the soul, in St. Augustine's *De Trinitate*. Despite all this, I failed to see the connection of this trinitarian theory with the *Anniversaries*. Fortunately scholarship is a communal adventure!

[20]Edward Dawson, "The Practical Methode of Meditation," prefixed to *An Abridgment of Meditations . . . Written in Italian by the R. Father Vincentius Bruno*, St. Omer, 1614. Dawson's treatise is reprinted in *The Anchor Anthology of Seventeenth-Century Verse* (see above, n. 18); this quotation comes from pp. 503-4.

[21]Nicolson, p. 65 (1950 edn.).

Louis L. Martz

A SELECTED BIBLIOGRAPHY OF WRITINGS ON DONNE'S *ANNIVERSARIES*
1942-1972

Richards, I. A. "The Interactions of Words." *The Language of Poetry*. Ed. Allen Tate. Princeton: Princeton University Press, 1942, pp. 65-87. Contains a significant defense of the poetical technique of the *First Anniversary*.

Martz, Louis L. "John Donne in Meditation: The *Anniversaries*." *ELH*, 14 (1947), 247-73. Incorporated in Martz's book *The Poetry of Meditation* (New Haven: Yale University Press, 1954), pp. 219-48, along with an Appendix, "The Dating and Significance of Donne's *Anniversaries*," pp. 353-6.

Nicolson, Marjorie Hope. *The Breaking of the Circle: Studies in the Effect of the "New Science" upon Seventeenth Century Poetry*. Evanston: Northwestern University Press, 1950; rev. edn. New York: Columbia University Press, 1960, Chap. 3: "The Death of a World."

Leishman, J. B. *The Monarch of Wit*. London: Hutchinson, 1951. See Chap. 5.

Allen, Don Cameron. "The Double Journey of John Donne." *A Tribute to George Coffin Taylor*. Ed. Arnold Williams. Chapel Hill: University of North Carolina Press, 1952, pp. 83-99. Deals with Donne's two "Progress" poems, *Metempsychosis* and *Second Anniversary*.

Bewley, Marius. "Religious Cynicism in Donne's Poetry." *Kenyon Review*, 14 (1952), 609-46. Argues that the *Anniversaries* deal with Donne's attitudes toward the Church.

Simon, Irène. *Some Problems of Donne Criticism*. Brussels: Didier, [1952], (*Langues Vivantes*, No. 40). A 76-page monograph that deserves to be more widely known; pages 29-47 contain a detailed analysis of the construction of the *Anniversaries*, considered as devotional exercises.

Cruttwell, Patrick. *The Shakespearean Moment and its Place in the Poetry of the 17th Century*. London: Chatto and Windus, 1954. Chapter 3 contains a careful interpretation of the *Anniversaries* (especially of the second) in relation to Shakespeare's last plays.

Maud, Ralph N. "Donne's *First Anniversary*." *Boston University Studies in English*, 2 (1956), 218-25.

Bald, R. C. *Donne and the Drurys*. Cambridge: Cambridge University Press, 1959. Important for biographical setting of the *Anniversaries*.

Hardison, O. B., Jr. *The Enduring Monument: A Study of the Idea of Praise in Renaissance Literary Theory and Practice*. Chapel Hill: University of North Carolina Press, 1962. Chapter 7, "The Idea of Elizabeth Drury," studies the *Anniversaries* "in the context of the theory of praise."

Williamson, George. "The Design of Donne's *Anniversaries*." *Modern Philology*, 60 (1963), 183-91. Included in Williamson's book *Milton and Others* (London: Faber and Faber,

1965), pp. 150-64. Opens with an attack on Martz's point of view, but then proceeds to develop some interesting ideas.

Manley, Frank, ed. *John Donne: The Anniversaries*. Baltimore: The Johns Hopkins Press, 1963. An excellent text with indispensable introduction and commentary.

Colie, Rosalie. "The Rhetoric of Transcendence." *Philological Quarterly*, 43 (1964), 145-70. Incorporated in Miss Colie's book, *Paradoxia Epidemica: The Renaissance Tradition of Paradox* (Princeton: Princeton University Press, 1966), Chap. 13. Divided into two parts: "I. Traditions of Paradox in Renaissance Verse-Epistemologies" and "II. John Donne's Anniversary Poems and the Paradoxes of Epistemology."

Love, Harold. "The Argument of Donne's *First Anniversary*." *Modern Philology*, 64 (1966), 125-31. An admirable correction of Martz's adverse view of the *Anatomy*.

Hughes, Richard E. "The Woman in Donne's *Anniversaries*." *ELH*, 34 (1967), 307-26. Incorporated in Hughes' book, *The Progress of the Soul: The Interior Career of John Donne* (New York: Morrow, 1968), Chap. 4. Presents the view that "St. Lucy was the energizing source of Donne's symbolism" in the *Anniversaries*.

Quinn, Dennis. "Donne's *Anniversaries* as Celebration." *Studies in English Literature*, 9 (1969), 97-105. Argues for the "public" nature of the poems.

Mahony, Patrick. "The *Anniversaries*: Donne's Rhetorical Approach to Evil." *Journal of English and Germanic Philology*, 68 (1969), 407-13. An important clarification of the meditative aspects of these poems.

Voss, A. E. "The Structure of Donne's *Anniversaries*." *English Studies in Africa*, 12 (1969), 1-30. An important essay, arguing that the unity and sequence of the poems are based on Donne's attitudes toward language and verse.

Miner, Earl. *The Metaphysical Mode from Donne to Cowley*. Princeton: Princeton University Press, 1969. Pages 59-75 present a sensitive and judicious study of the *Anniversaries* from the standpoint of Donne's "thematic treatment of time."

Sicherman, Carol M. "Donne's Timeless *Anniversaries*." *University of Toronto Quarterly*, 39 (1970), 127-43. A remarkably perceptive essay, with fair and tactful allusion to previous writings on the subject.

Anselment, Raymond A. " 'Ascensio Mendax, Descensio Crudelis': The Image of Babel in the *Anniversaries*." *ELH*, 38 (1971), 188-205.

Benson, Donald R. "Platonism and Neoclassic Metaphor: Dryden's *Eleonora* and Donne's *Anniversaries*." *Studies in Philology*, 68 (1971), 340-56.

Fox, Ruth A. "Donne's *Anniversaries* and the Art of Living." *ELH*, 38 (1971), 528-41.

Stanwood, P. G. " 'Essentiall Joye' in Donne's *Anniversaries*." *Texas Studies in Literature and Language*, 13 (1971), 227-38.

Crawshaw, Eluned. "Hermetic Elements in Donne's Poetic Vision." *John Donne: Essays in Celebration*. Ed. A. J.

Smith. London: Methuen, 1972, pp. 324-48. Contains many useful comments on the *Anniversaries*.

Mahony, Patrick. "The Structure of Donne's *Anniversaries* as Companion Poems." *Genre*, 5 (1972), 235-56. Deals with "the detailed parallelism between the corresponding sections of each poem."

Patricia G. Pinka

THE AUTOBIOGRAPHICAL NARRATOR IN THE
SONGS AND SONNETS

Within John Donne's *Songs and Sonnets* stands a small
group of poems in the narrative mode. Antithetical in technique
to the dramatic encounter of most of the *Songs and Sonnets*,
these lyrics present a speaker relating his autobiography either to
an unnamed, rather impersonal audience or to a specific listener
ignorant of the narrator's facts. The dramatic vigor of the face-
to-face confrontation gives way to the more subdued atmosphere
of a storyteller relating a yarn or a speaker addressing a formal
audience. The reader's interest shifts from the situation of the
poem to the story narrated and to the reporter himself. Moreover,
since the narrator in each of these poems tells *his own* story, the
distinction between tale and teller fades, and the reader focuses
his attention on the speaker. For it is through the reporter that
Donne manipulates the complexities latent in any literary work
with a narrator, complexities which arise from what we call in the
novel "point of view."

Every autobiographical narrator in the *Songs and Sonnets*
espouses an extreme view of love, advocating either hedonistic
dissipation, Platonic restraint, or an idealized fiction so ethereal
that it can be explained only in negative terms. They all speak,
in other words, from a biased standpoint. Other speakers in the
Songs and Sonnets intersperse some narrative in their dramatic
encounters—the fiction of the ghost who will return to haunt the

fickle woman in "The Apparition," for example—but in poems such as these, the fiction is subsumed by the dramatic confrontation. Only speakers with extreme views of love rely solely on the narrative mode and, moreover, use that mode to present their autobiographies—either a record of their philosophical positions, their experiences, or their beliefs about their own spiritual worth. Since, as Scholes and Kellogg tell us, autobiography itself contains the potential for fabrication, is indeed derived from the tradition of the Traveler's tale, which has evolved into our "fish" story, the very fact that these particular speakers choose to narrate their own stories arouses suspicions about their reliability.[1] When one adds to this generic doubt the fact that all the autobiographical reporters advocate views of love which diverge from a generally accepted norm that a healthy love relationship contains physical, spiritual, and psychological elements, and when one adds again to this consideration Donne's own propensity for satire, it becomes evident that Donne is manipulating the technique of a narrator for all its potential, ironic entanglements. He sets up, in other words, each speaker's coherent fiction about love and asks the reader to sift that fiction through the intellectual strainers of his own experience and of his understanding of the narrator himself. Within the extremely concise space of each lyric, Donne provides enough clues for the reader to form an adequate judgment. It is possible in some of the poems which advocate hedonism to arrive at a similar conclusion about the speaker by noting his use of the fallacious syllogism to justify his beliefs, and a number of critics have done just this.[2] But Donne's manipulation of the autobiographical narrator pervades more of the lyrics than those built on a syllogism; and even when a speaker structures his utterance as a logical equation, his reliance on the methods of deductive reasoning helps characterize him as a seemingly

58

learned, very rational man. Donne, in other words, sets the reporter's version of himself in collision with the discrepancies and ironies which arise from the reporter's performance as a narrator. He juxtaposes the information which the speaker consciously relates to his listener with information about the reporter which he had not really intended to convey. For example, the speaker in the hedonistic poem "Communitie" consciously attempts to present himself as a reasonable and a moral man, both by structuring his utterance as a logical syllogism and by opening his speech with a moral maxim. Yet his syllogism is fallacious and his most striking comparison for a woman is that of a nutmeat to be devoured and cast aside:

> Chang'd loves are but chang'd sorts of meat,
> And when hee hath the kernell eate,
>   Who doth not fling away the shell?[3]

The reader, then, finds that the reporter's version of himself as a moral and reasonable man jars with his actions: his illusion of rationality vanishes as he cloaks his desires in the garb of logic; his illusion of morality disappears as he licks his lips in preparation for the delicious female morsels he will devour. Although all the examples are not so glaring as "Communitie," every autobiographical narrator describes himself quite differently from the way he presents himself.

A second factor arising from Donne's use of the autobiographical narrative centers on the unequal relationship between the speaker and his listener. In those poems built on the dramatic encounter, Donne assumes more or less an equality between speaker and listener: they are both involved in a face-to-face response to a particular situation, and the speaker values his listener's ideas and emotions enough to react to them, sometimes, as in "A Valediction: of Weeping," to participate in them.[4] In the poems which a reporter narrates, however, the speaker becomes the authority. He either reduces his listener to an "ear," which may indeed be a mere sounding board by which he justifies his ideas to himself, or he instructs or informs an untutored listener. In either case, the distance between the speaker and listener is magnified by the speaker's insistence upon his authority, his knowledge. In fact, one comes away from reading some of these lyrics with the sense that physical as well as psychological or intellectual distance separates the speaker and listener, as if the speaker were standing on a podium lecturing to a group of the uninitiated. This sense of distance accounts, in part, for the anonymity of the listener in a poem such as "Communitie." Ironically, these authoritarian narrators present information only about themselves; further, the more dogmatic the narrator, the more glaring the discrepancies in his account of himself, as if Donne were satirizing man's feeble attempts to cover his blindness with the power of convincing speech or his insecurity with vaunting. In these cases the autobiographer must somehow create the illusion that he is superior to his audience; he does so most effectively by remaining aloof from them, by treating them as anonymous entities. Even the autobiographical narrators whose assertiveness is tempered and who speak to clearly identified listeners treat those listeners as ears, or perhaps sounding boards; and, as in Browning's dramatic monologues, the autobiographer finally speaks to himself. This fading of the listener occurs in even such a tender lyric as "The Relique" where the "you" by which the woman is first addressed modulates to "shee" as the form of the speaker's fiction removes her from a rhetorical relationship with it.

A third factor arising from Donne's use of the autobiographical narrator concerns time. As I have implied, the narrative differs from the dramatic method of presentation in great part because the events of the narrative occur at a time other than the moment of the narration: usually the past, but in several of the *Songs and Sonnets* in a predestined future which the reporter sees developing. Drama unfolds in the present time before the eyes of the spectator. Hence, the very nature of narration allows for the possibility of an incorrect reporting of events—a possibility which is increased by the presence of an autobiographical narrator. Time discussed in this manner impinges on the earlier topic of point of view. However, another, more philosophical, considera-tion about the relationship between the speaker and time corre-lates in the *Songs and Sonnets* with the dramatic or narrative mode of presentation. In the dramatic poems, especially those which contain a face-to-face encounter, the speaker is absorbed in his intense momentary situation. For the time being, the mo-ment becomes his "all" and frequently pulls into it his past and begins the momentum toward his future. In such diverse poems as "Womans Constancy" and "The Anniversarie" the profound completeness of the moment vibrates throughout by frequent ref-erences to particular time. "Womans Constancy" begins with an explicit mention of the instant, projecting the present of the poem into the speaker's future: *"Now* thou hast lov'd me *one whole day,* / *To morrow* when thou leav'st, what wilt thou say?" (p. 42, italics mine). And "The Anniversarie" brings into its present the culmination of a year's relationship and the projection of fifty-nine more years of love on earth and an infinity of heavenly bliss. The speaker says that everything in the world "Is elder by a yeare, now, then it was / *When thou and I first one another saw*" (p. 71, italics mine). With the specific "now" reinforced by the explicitly delineated moment of meeting, "When thou and I first one another saw," he affirms the consuming importance of the present for him. The power of the moment transcends time for the speaker because it encompasses both his past and his future. To the autobiographical narrators, however, the present moment of their narration merely affords them an opportunity to return to their past or to project a future for themselves. It holds no potential in itself. The Platonic lover in "The Relique" looks to the future to reward him for his present abstention from sexual fulfillment. He says:

> *then*
> Thou shalt be'a Mary Magdalen, and I
> A something else thereby;
> All women shall adore us, and some men.
> (p. 90, italics mine)

The hedonists in both "Communitie" and "Confined Love" return to the past to justify their philosophical views about lust, seeing themselves caught in a dilemma which is not of their making. In "Communitie" the speaker exonerates himself by blaming the past:

> If then *at first* wise Nature *had*
> Made women either good or bad,
> *Then* some wee might hate, and some chuse.
> (pp. 33-34, italics mine)

His careful arrangement of time on a cause-and-effect line, "If . . . at first . . . Then . . . we might," makes clear that he sees his present as an almost fatalistic completion of forces set in motion in the past, forces beyond his control. These examples come from totally narrative poems; but in every one of the *Songs and Sonnets* which contains a narrative at all, the speaker clutches to his fiction to help him withstand, explain, or justify some aspect of his present. In "A Valediction: of my Name in the Window" he projects that his signature engraved in the window of his beloved's house will send magic spells over her and keep her faithful to him while he is gone, for he sees in his departure the potential disintegration of their love. In "The Apparition" the speaker resorts to the threat of his spectral haunting to punish his unfaithful mistress, for in the present moment of the poem he is helpless. She has been unfaithful to him; he has called her names; and yet he is unsatisfied. In "A Valediction: forbidding Mourning" the fiction that the lovers' souls are like a pair of drawing compasses helps the speaker contain his own fears about parting and helps him ease his beloved's apprehension. The narrative of the "Extasie" justifies the lover's request to "turn to bodies"; the fiction of the sanctioning of the lovers in "The Canonization" vindicates the speaker's rejection of the world. In the *Songs and Sonnets*, then, the narrative mode marks the speaker's uneasiness with his present in some degree or another. In the poems which are totally narrative, the speaker's rejection of his present moment is so complete that he turns either to the past or the future to transcend it.

These three factors—the narrator's point of view, his relationship to his listener, and his movement away from the present—subtly interweave to modify the meanings of the autobiographical narratives in the *Songs and Sonnets*. A detailed look at several of the poems will exemplify the interaction of these elements.

The hedonist-turned-ascetic who speaks "Farewell to Love" (pp. 82-83) traces his own disillusioning experiences with sex as proof that the only rational approach to "love" is abstention. He offers a first person testimonial to his listeners as an *exemplum*,

teaching them from his own encounters of the essentially deceptive nature of love and of the consuming emptiness which he has
experienced after each sexual relationship. He has, then, an "axe
to grind," so to speak: he wants to prove that the physical urge
which he terms love is essentially deceptive and can be overcome
by will power and rational analysis. Further he hopes to convert
his listeners to his own resolution to refrain from sexual activity
altogether (if we can term "resolution" a conclusion which carries
an "if" clause: "If all faile, / 'Tis but applying worme-seed to the
Taile.").

In order to persuade his listeners of the validity of his ideas,
the narrator sprinkles his language with many phrases and terms
from logic: "Whilst yet to prove," "Unlesse wise / Nature de-
creed," and "Since so." Moreover, he categorizes his particular
experience of blindly worshipping love as an example of the falla-
cies which arise when men let their imagination not their reason
control their actions:

> Thus when
> Things not yet knowne are coveted by men,
> Our desires give them fashion, and so
> As they waxe lesser, fall, as they sise, grow.

Further he shapes his narrative as a tale of hope, despair, and
redemption—a pattern markedly similar to the comic-Christian
cycle of salvation, sin, and redemption—as if to suggest that the
paradigm itself points up both the logical and the religious validity of his solution to the physical dilemma of lust. He even hunts
for a scientific explanation of his satiety with the sexual act,
settling on the idea that nature made man's sexual appetite cloy
as a means of self preservation, and emphatically declares that
he bases *his own* resolution to abstain from sexual relations on

just that scientific fact.

Yet in spite of this rational gloss, discrepancies protrude into his performance. The first consists of his subtle equation of reason and appetite. Explaining that as a young man he tried to test the proposition that love is a god, he says, "Whilst yet to prove, / I thought there was some Deitie in love." Yet he describes this intellectual pursuit in terms applicable only to desire: "As ignorantly did I crave." The fact that he characterizes his old craving self as ignorant should imply that his present self is enlightened. However, the enlightened self never questions the suitability of treating desire and reason as one, for he begins the final stanza of the poem by describing his resolution with precisely the same paradoxical linkage: "Since so, my minde / Shall not desire." The second discrepancy in the narrator's image of himself as a rational man occurs through his unwitting revelation of self-pity, almost childish self-pity. He wants to present himself as *dis*illusioned, i.e., knowledgeable, as his heavy reliance on the terminology of logical propositions indicates. His analogies, however, shift this image to one of a man indulging, even wallowing, in pity for his own helplessness, his own victimization. By comparing himself when he worshipped love to the dying atheist who blindly prays to an unknown power and by depicting his sexual attraction in terms of a child's yearning for a glittering gingerbread man at a fair, the narrator portrays himself as an innocent duped. Through these comparisons he indicates that he was "taken in" by romantic notions of love which proved untrue in his experience. Thus he links pity for his innocence with loathing for his sexual encounters until the love-hate ambivalence for himself stagnates into a tension. Instead of trying to resolve his conflict, he projects his hatred outward onto the sexual act itself, which he terms that "*thing* which lovers so / Blindly admire, and with such worship wooe" (italics mine). In his vitriolic accusation of love as the cause of his disgust and satiation, however, he inadvertently lashes out at himself; for he was one of those lovers who "Blindly admire, and with such worship wooe." The pity he felt for himself in his early experiences with love twists into mockery and self-hatred in the speaker's confusion; and in spite of himself he half acknowledges that his disgust arises from himself, not from the sexual act. His carefully chosen words quite obviously omit mention of the human actor in physical union:

> Being had, enjoying it decayes:
> And thence,
> What before pleas'd them all, takes but one sense,
> And that so lamely, as it leaves behinde
> A kinde of sorrowing dulnesse to the minde.

Although his disembodied version of lustful satiety suggests his fear to acknowledge his participation in such behavior, his self scorn vibrates through the sibilance in the passage. A third discrepancy in the narrator's autobiography arises from his hasty generalizations—a point which I shall take up in a few moments.

Even though the listeners in "Farewell to Love" are unnamed nonentities, the speaker comes before them to persuade them of the validity of his ideas. We have noticed how carefully he creates the illusion that he is a very rational man—an image designed to underscore his authority. In addition he makes several attempts to equate his experiences with those of his listeners, as if to intimate that his conclusions should be theirs. His reference back to common or shared experience, such as the notion that the imagination can puff an idea out of proportion, creates a bridge of identification between himself and his listeners. They can say, "Ah, ha, just that sort of thing happened to me once

66

too." Thus they are more inclined to believe in him or identify with him. After his first reference to the imagination, the speaker pushes his rhetorical identification with the listeners only at those spots where his conclusions about sensuality are shakiest. The next time he asks for the consent of his audience, his subject touches the very heart of the question: What is the nature of man? Having detailed at length the dulling satiety which cloys him after each sexual encounter, the narrator wistfully asks:

> Ah cannot wee,
> As well as Cocks and Lyons jocund be,
> After such pleasures?

He refers, of course, to the belief that both of these animals were exempt from post-coital depression; he implies that since man is superior to all beasts, he should be entitled to at least as much pleasure as they. Using the rhetorical question to achieve the illusion of consent, he pushes his listeners to agree to his wish that a man might enjoy unbridled sexual delight as the cock and lion do. His "wee" makes his desire theirs as well. Lying right behind that wish is the whole issue of man's difference from the beasts—a subject which broaches the morality and spirituality of man's every action and which contains the hierarchy of the faculties within man himself. To shut out this entire area of consideration, the narrator pretends to request affirmation. If his listeners agree with him, the subject is closed. Ironically, the rhetorical question, often used to ensnare an audience, becomes the means by which the narrator deludes himself. Through it he can pretend to ask the listeners for their assent and pretend to receive it. He can imagine that he and his audience speak with one voice. Only once more in the poem does the narrator reach for an identification with his hearers, in the overgeneralization I alluded to a few minutes ago. After he has decided that abstinence is the only solution to his licentious loathing, he proclaims: "Since so, *my minde / Shall not desire what no man else* can finde" (italics mine). If he can convince himself that his disgust with sexual encounters is universal, he can easily denounce "love" altogether; and by subsuming his individual response into the experience of all men, he can avoid examining his personal conclusions. If no other man can find satisfaction in "love," why should he expect to?

The listeners in "Farewell to Love," then, become both ears and sounding boards for the speaker. Even though they are non-entities, he must convince them of the rightness of his ideas, must elicit their support for his views, so that their affirmation will keep him from inquiring whether his own propositions are correct.

As the speaker's insistence on his listeners' assent implies, the present for the narrator in "Farewell to Love" merely affords him an opportunity to justify the past and to project a future based on the experiences of the past. In one sense, the present for the narrator is an inactive time—a pause in which he uncritically, almost wistfully, reflects upon the past and asserts his future course of action. Ironically, the present of the poem contains that very activity which should most absorb the speaker, were he really the intensely reasoning man of his self-portrait: logical deduction. But he is no such thing.

With the exception of a single sentence, the first three stanzas in "Farewell to Love" depict the past: the speaker's innocent worship of love, his disillusionment, and in some very distant time, Nature's decree that men should grow sated with sexual intercourse for self-preservation. The fourth and final stanza of the poem formulates the speaker's future. He almost omits the present. As the poem opens he recreates for the audience the self

68

he once was, an idealistic young man ensnared by romantic notions of the almost religious power of love:

> Whilst yet to prove,
> I thought there was some Deitie in love,
> So did I reverence, and gave
> Worship, as Atheists at their dying houre
> Call, what they cannot name, an unknowne power,
> As ignorantly did I crave.

The description, with its suggestions of helplessness arising out of the analogy, indicates that the speaker still laments the loss of his innocent self: the young man who was involved, excited, caught up in a wonderful idea, who "did . . . reverence," "gave/ Worship," and "did . . . crave." The very subtle pun on "dying hour" reminds us and perhaps the speaker himself just how far he has moved from that innocence. The future self of the fourth stanza will participate no more; in fact he adamantly will avoid any kind of encounter. He says, "I'll no more dote and runne / To pursue things which had, indammage me," and sees his course of action as "shunning." As his melodramatic autobiography runs, everything worthwhile belongs either to the past or the future. In only two sentences of the whole poem does the speaker attempt to structure a "now" at all, and even these partake more of a conditional and wistful present than the temporal moment. After he has expanded upon the satiety he experiences after intercourse, he asks:

> Ah cannot wee,
> As well as Cocks and Lyons jocund be,
> After such pleasures?

He is yearning that men might be more vigorously animalistic, that sexual experience might be free from morality and commitment. A present so defined would consume him. He ends his utterance with another wishful definition, which might make his life acceptable, were it true. Having elaborated on his resolve to abstain from intercourse if at all possible, he adds an afterthought: "If all faile, / 'Tis but applying worme-seed to the Taile." Even though the "it" in "'Tis" has no clear antecedent in the poem, by context it refers to the physical union itself; and the speaker minimizes the experience by equating it with an anaphrodisiac, "worme-seed." After all, he tries to convince himself, a physical relationship serves only to lessen sexual desire, nothing more. If the present were as he wishes, the speaker would be happy.

The autobiographical narrator in "Farewell to Love," then, manipulates his listeners by trying to convince them of his acutely honed rationality; for he depends very much on their acceptance of him and their agreement with his ideas. Without their support, he might have to question his conclusions; and then he might see through the fabric of his own disguise. Moreover, he is so consumed with justifying himself that he expends his life vindicating his past and rationalizing his future.

In "The Relique" (pp. 89-90), a poem far removed in statement from "Farewell to Love," the speaker also manipulates the meaning of his utterance through his careful handling of point of view, through his relationship with his listener, and through his movement away from the present. The narrator, an avowed Platonic lover, recounts to his beloved their future after death, or more specifically the future of "his" bones, one of which will be encircled with a lock of "her" hair. Through the bones and a note which the speaker will have enclosed in the grave, both he and his beloved will attain renown for their miraculous Platonic relationship. The poem presents, in short, a spectral autobiography of lovers who become saints because they did not consummate their love.

Because the narrator's vision of himself is embedded in his fictions about the future, he, in one way, cares less about presenting himself to his immediate listener, his beloved, than about making a good appearance before his future listeners, the fictional gravedigger who exhumes his body, the imagined bishop and king to whom his remains will be taken, and the unknown, future generation who will read his chronicle on the paper found in his grave. Of course, the woman hears his fictions and overhears the praise of her in the note intended for the ears of future generations; and part of the tension in the poem arises from the question of how fully the speaker manipulates his fictions in order to influence her.

As he presents himself to his listeners, both present and future, the narrator creates conflicting impressions, both of which grow from the ambiguity of the relic itself. For the "bracelet of bright haire about the bone" creates both the figure of the theta and the image of sexual union. As a theta, first letter in Greek *Thanatos*, the "bracelet of bright haire" figures forth the speaker's mortality and his immortality—a combination which the concept of relic implies. As a symbol of sexual union, however, the "bracelet of bright haire" conflicts with the speaker's accolades about his Platonic relationship with his beloved, more so because the gravedigger, the bishop, and the king all misread the relic as a sign that the two were either lovers or Christ and Mary Magdalen in their fictional roles as lovers. That is to say, because of the ambiguity of the relic the speaker has created a spectral autobiography "open" for misinterpretation. Moreover, he hints that in some way this mistaken autobiography fulfills a genuine

71

desire for him; for he imagines himself responding to the intruding gravedigger with a lover's wish for intimate seclusion in the tomb:

> Will he not let'us alone,
> And thinke that there a loving couple lies,
> Who thought that this device might be some way
> To make their soules, at the last busie day,
> Meet at this grave, and make a little stay?

The lover of the fictional gravedigger's imagination participates in a deep and devoted relationship with his beloved, seeing in their physical union a symbol of their spiritual union: a lover who "thought that this device might be some way / To make their *soules* . . . / Meet at this grave" (italics mine). Ironically it is this "self" who becomes the idol in a land of mis-devotion, and the speaker first gains his immortality as a saint on false grounds: he is worshipped as a great lover, when indeed he was no such thing.

The speaker's second image of himself unfolds through his own note which clarifies the meaning of the relic and sets straight the intriguing misinterpretation it propagated. In this view he is a saint because he miraculously managed to keep his love relationship free from sexual involvement. He twice refers to his life with his beloved as a series of miracles, events which contradict natural law; and by writing a saint's legend of their lives together, he is seeking the reward due to one who performs miracles, recognition. Ironically, however, he is both the chronicler of and the actor in the legend.

The speaker's two images of himself complicate his celebration of Platonic love by mingling with it a vision of consummated love. Moreover, the commemoration is colored by his gnawing desire to have public recognition for his private actions—an indiscretion, indeed an infringement, on the sanctity of the relationship, as his own repudiation of the gravedigger's intrusion makes clear. For through his enigmatic relic the speaker has fostered the misinterpretation of his love for the woman, and even his clarification of their bonds exposes their intimacy. Since the revelation will occur in the future, however, long after the speaker and his beloved are dead, the suggestion of violation is mollified.

And it is the future to which the reporter in "The Relique" has committed himself. More startlingly, even, than the narrator of "Farewell to Love," the narrator in "The Relique" rejects the present. By structuring the early stanzas of the poem on a "When . . . then" contingency and by speaking of the future in the present tense, he obliterates the present almost entirely. In the final stanza he even discusses his present existence in the past tense, putting the spontaneity and shapelessness of experience into the chiseled form of art. For the speaker in "The Relique," the future holds his chance for reward. Through the symbol of his love with his lady, the "bracelet of bright haire about the bone," he hopes to gain immortality and finally recognition for his miraculous endeavor. He is saying, in other words, that wonderful as his beloved is, the present experience of their relationship is really not enough. He clearly seeks a means, albeit a tenuous one, to let others know what he has endured, to let them praise him for his ability to thwart nature, and to let them admire the woman for whom he has accomplished these feats.

The speaker's relationship with his audience in "The Relique" is compounded by the fact that he addresses, at once, listeners far separated by time and custom. Although the narrative of his exhuming originally is directed to his beloved, as soon as the speaker becomes involved in his story, his thoughts and words are aimed at the people of future generations, until by the end of the poem he is reciting to his beloved a note intended for the eyes of future generations. Instead of being his listener, she becomes primarily the subject of the paper and only secondarily a listener, or more correctly an overhearer. That is to say, progressively throughout "The Relique" the speaker distances himself from his beloved by moving his narrative farther and farther from her, while still celebrating her. The only grammatical structure even close to direct address in the poem depicts her future identity: "then / Thou shalt be'a Mary Magdalen, and I / A something else thereby." I surely stretch the grammar a bit to find this sentence so emphatic; but I can imagine the speaker gesturing to his listener here, calling her into the narration by mentioning her individually. This reference to "thou" is the only occasion in the "narrated," as opposed to "read," section of the poem where the woman's identity is separated from the speaker's. Elsewhere he refers to her as "us" or as half of "a loving couple." In the paper to future generations, the woman becomes "shee."

This distancing between the speaker and his listener perhaps indicates that in the poem his relationship to her is different from that of lover to beloved. As lover, he would confront her directly. In the poem, however, he is an autobiographer, then a chronicler—variations of the concept of poet as singer, whose task is to celebrate not encounter. Moreover, as he moves from autobiographer to chronicler within the poem—moves, that is, into an aesthetic distance from his subject material—his commemoration both of his love and of his lady intensifies. The discrepancies between the speaker's images of himself as a lover and his celebration of a Platonic relationship perhaps reflect this progression in his roles. As autobiographer he is only one step removed from his "life." He tells his tale directly to his beloved, looks at her as

74

he speaks. Of course, then, he is emotionally involved in his story. As chronicler, however, he is the all-knowing artist, intellectually aware both of the magnificence of the Platonic relationship and of the miraculous restraint required to perpetrate it. Only when the speaker has fully immersed himself in the role of chronicler, when he reads from the paper he has written, do his images of sexual union disappear. Only then is he able objectively to define their relationship as a miracle, one which goes against nature: "Our hands ne'r toucht the seales, / Which nature, injur'd by late law, sets free."

This objectivity, however, entails the loss of involvement with his love experiences. Instead he turns to his work as an artist, bemoaning in part his limitations as poet in the final lines of the poem: "but now alas, / All *measure*, and all *language*, I should passe, / Should I tell what a miracle shee was" (italics mine). Like the woman, the speaker changes his rhetorical relationship to the material in the paper from which he reads. He also listens to it, scrutinizingly, and ironically becomes objective about the relationship which the note describes so that he can be scrutinizing about the artistic rendering of that relationship. He wants to hear what it "sounds like." But with Donne's usual ability for wrenching irony out of irony, it is through the speaker's "artistic" re-creation of his beloved that he discovers (or rediscovers) that indeed she is too good for words.

The narrator in "The Relique" comes to appreciate both his beloved and their love fully, only when he has rendered them into art, when he has removed his personal involvement from them. Until then his own needs push through his attempts at celebration as he searches for recognition in spectral fantasies. Once he has transformed the present into shaped narrative, he can transcend his day-to-day existence and truly commemorate the value

75

of his love.

The autobiographical narratives within the *Songs and Sonnets*, then, remind us of Donne's richness as a lyric poet. Perhaps our own twentieth-century bias about the significance of the encounter, the importance of the confrontation, and the meaning of the dramatic experience has turned our attention to Donne's acute rendering of the dramatic moment and cast our eyes aside from Donne's skill in handling the narrative mode as well. In the best of his autobiographical narratives, he has fused the complexities of the dramatic encounter with the intriguing possibilities of an involved interpreter.

Notes:

[1]Robert Scholes and Robert Kellogg, *The Nature of Narrative* (New York: Oxford University Press, 1966), p. 73.

[2]See, for example, Thomas O. Sloan, "The Rhetoric in the Poetry of John Donne," *Studies in English Literature, 1500-1900*, 3 (1963), 31-44, or Elizabeth Lewis Wiggins, "Logic in the Poetry of John Donne," *Studies in Philology*, 42 (1945), 41-60.

[3]John Donne, *The Elegies and The Songs and Sonnets*, ed. Helen Gardner (Oxford: The Clarendon Press, 1965), p. 34. All other citations are to this edition.

[4]See Earl Miner's discussion of the relationship between the speaker and the listener in *The Metaphysical Mode from Donne to Cowley* (Princeton: Princeton University Press, 1969), p. 178.

SEVENTEENTH CENTURY MUSIC FOR LUTE AND VOICE

Sally Martin, Soprano
Louis Aull, Lutenist

Agnes Scott College
February 25, 1972

PROGRAM

DONNE SONGS

'Tis True, 'Tis Day, What Though It Be?
(Breake of Day)   William Corkine

First printed in Corkine's *Second Booke of Ayres*, 1612. Lute
part arranged by André Souris.

Send Home My Longe Strayde Eies to Mee
(The Message)   Giovanni Coperario
(John Cooper, c. 1575-1626)

In MS. Tenbury 1019. Lute part arranged by André Souris.
Coperario composed music for masques and was musical instructor to the sons of James I.

Sweetest Love, I Do Not Goe   Anonymous

In MS. Tenbury 1018. Lute part arranged by André Souris.

Miss Martin and Mr. Aull

FANTASIE   Gregorio Huwet

Huwet was a lutenist to the Duke of Brunswick, and is men-
tioned with respect and affection by the celebrated seventeenth century English composer of airs, John Dowland.

Mr. Aull

77

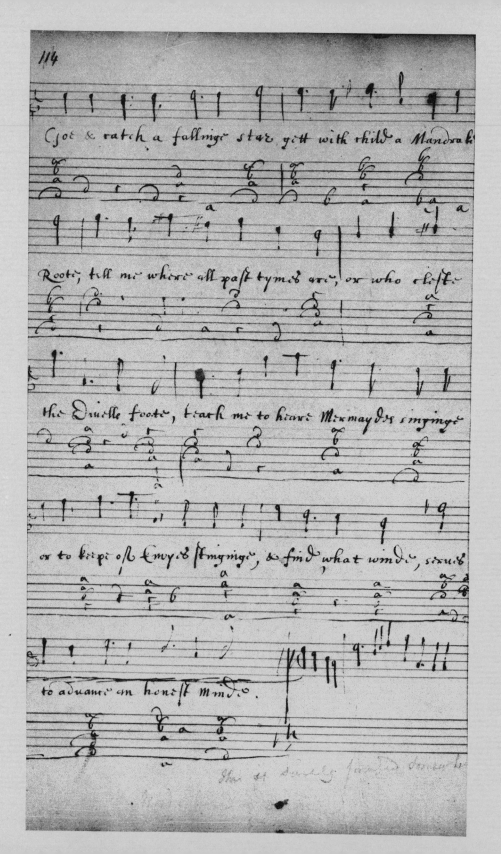

Goe & catch a fallinge star, gett with child a Mandrake

Roote, tell me where all past tymes are, or who cleste

the Diuelle foote, teach me to heare Mermaydes singinge

or to keepe of Envyes stinginge, & find what winde, serues

to aduance an honest Minde.

DONNE SONGS

So, So, Breake Off this Last Lamenting Kisse
(The Expiration)

a.   Anonymous

From Bodleian MS. Mus. Sch. 575.

b.   Alfonso Ferrabosco
                                    the Younger
                                     (d. 1628)

From Ferrabosco's *First Book of Ayres* (1609). Ferrabosco was
noted as a lutenist and composer, and was musical instructor
to Prince Henry.

Wilt Thou Forgive that Sinne Where I Begunne
(Hymne to God the Father)   John Hilton
                                   (d. 1657)

Appearing in British Museum MS. Egerton 2013, with setting
for voice and bass viol; the lute part has been arranged by
André Souris. John Hilton was organist of St. Margaret's,
Westminster, until organs were suppressed in 1644.

Miss Martin and Mr. Aull

A NOTE ON THE MUSIC

Exhibited at the Quatercentenary Celebration were photocopies of Donne's "The
Expiration," set to music for lute and voice by Alfonso Ferrabosco in his *First Book of
Ayres* (1609), and "Goe and Catch a Fallinge Star," the latter reproduced from British
Museum MS. Egerton 2013, f.58 v and included in this volume by permission of the British
Library Board.

For arrangements of the songs performed at the Celebration, thanks were due the
Centre National de la Recherche scientifique in Paris, which granted permission to photo-
copy for the use of the performers pages of the Centre National publication, *Poèmes de
Donne, Herbert et Crashaw mis en musique par leurs contemporains*, Transcription et
réalisation par André Souris, Introduction par Jean Jacquot (1961).

This program was planned and prepared by Professor Margret G. Trotter of the
English department, assisted by Professor Theodore Mathews of the Music department
who directed musical aspects of the program.

FRANK MANLEY, Professor of English, Emory University, is the editor of *John Donne: The Anniversaries* (The Johns Hopkins Press), editor of George Chapman's *All Fools* (Regents Renaissance Drama Series), and co-editor and translator of Richard Pace, *De Fructu qui ex Doctrina Percipitur* (Renaissance Society of America). He is working with Professor Louis L. Martz, editing St. Thomas More's "Dialogue of Comfort" for the *Works of St. Thomas More* (Yale University Press). Professor Manley taught at The Johns Hopkins and Yale universities before joining the Emory faculty in 1964.

LOUIS L. MARTZ, Director of the Beinecke Rare Book and Manuscript Library and Sterling Professor of English at Yale University, is responsible for some of the most significant recent scholarship on John Donne. In 1955 he won the Christian Gauss Prize of Phi Beta Kappa for *The Poetry of Meditation: A Study in English Religious Literature of the 17th Century* (Yale University Press), and he is the author of *The Paradise Within: Studies in Vaughan, Traherne, and Milton* (Yale University Press). He serves on the editorial board of the Yale edition of *Complete Prose Works of John Milton* and is chairman of the editorial board of the Yale edition of *Works of St. Thomas More.* Professor Martz has been a member of the Yale faculty since 1938.

PATRICIA G. PINKA, Assistant Professor of English, Agnes Scott College, was an Andrew Mellon Fellow, 1967-68, and earned the Ph. D. degree from the University of Pittsburgh in 1969. Her dissertation, "The Voices in John Donne's *Songs and Sonnets,*" is now being prepared for publication. She taught at Point Park College and the University of Pittsburgh before joining the Agnes Scott faculty in 1969.